ABANDONED into ABUNDANCE

ALEDA J. MARSHALL

COPYRIGHTS

All Scripture quotations from the Holy Bible, King James Version (KJV), PUBLIC DOMAIN

All Scripture quotations unless otherwise indicated are taken from The Holy Bible, New International Version® NIV® Copyright © 1973 1978 1984 2011 by Biblica, Inc. ™ Used by permission. All rights reserved worldwide.

Scriptures marked as "(THE MESSAGE)" are Scripture quotations from THE MESSAGE. Copyright (c) by Eugene H.Peterson 1993, 1994, 1995, 1996, 2000, 2001, 2002. Used by permission of NavPress Publishing Group.

Italics in Scripture notations indicate the author's added emphasis. Details in some anecdotes and stories have been changed to protect the identities of the persons involved.

All rights reserved. No part of this book may be reproduced or utilized in any form or by any means, electronic or mechanical, including photocopying or recording, or by any information storage and retrieval system, without permission in writing from the author.

The author has made a sincere attempt to acknowledge the different authors and respective works. However, if any omission of acknowledgement has occurred, we will gladly rectify the matter in future editions.

Published For:

HE and ME MINISTRIES
307 ½ 3RD Ave NW #116
Roseau, Mn 56751

Copyright © 2013 ALEDA J MARSHALL

All rights reserved.

ISBN-13: 978-1490354255
ISBN-10: 1490354255

ABOUT THE AUTHOR

Aleda J Marshall is an inspirational Christian author whose writings provide choice keys to unlock doors of personal adversity and treasure keys to press on with abundance of purpose. She began writing and compiling Bible tracts in 2008. When not visiting the elderly in her community, facilitating electronic prayer requests, or leading Growth Groups, Ms. Marshall enjoys the meditation and study of the Word of God. She accepted Jesus as her Lord and Savior in 1976. It has been a bumpy road, but God promised to never leave or forsake her. After divorce, Ms. Marshall returned to college to attain her Bachelor of Science Degree in Business Administration, Major: Accounting from the University of Minnesota, graduating in 1989. She also has a Masters of Accounting Degree from Nova Southeastern University. In 2016, Aleda graduated from Gulf Coast Bible Training Center and is now a licensed international minister.

Other books include:

NO, NEVER ALONE "I PROMISED"
Copyright © 2012 ALEDA J. MARSHALL, All rights reserved.
ISBN-13:978-1475111101   ISBN-10: 14751111101

LAND of the HOMELESS BRAVE
Copyright © 2012 ALEDA J. MARSHALL, 2nd EDITION. All rights reserved. ISBN-13: 978-1475196115 ISBN-10: 1475196113

STILL STANDING "Equipped Grounded Praying"
Copyright ©2012 ALEDA J. MARSHALL, All rights reserved.
ISBN-13:978-1475194173   ISBN-10: 147519417X

ARE YOU SPEAKING "LIFE" or "DEATH"
Copyright ©2013 ALEDA J. MARSHALL, All rights reserved.
ISBN-13:978-1481201582   ISBN-10: 1481201581

ANOINTED WITH COURAGE
Copyright ©2013 ALEDA J. MARSHALL, All rights reserved.
ISBN-13:978-1482695335   ISBN-10: 1482695332

HUSBAND "forgive me"
Copyright ©2012 ALEDA J. MARSHALL, All rights reserved.
ISBN-13:978-1481115216 ISBN-10: 1481115219

ABBA, my FATHER
Copyright ©2013 ALEDA J. MARSHALL, All rights reserved.
ISBN-13:978-1490970578   ISBN-10: 1490970576

FLOURISHING FORGIVENESS
Copyright ©2014 ALEDA J. MARSHALL, All rights reserved.
ISBN-13: 978-1497331266 ISBN-10: 1497331269

TENT OF WITNESS
Copyright ©2014 ALEDA J MARSHALL, All rights reserved.
ISBN-13: 978-1502741622 ISBN-10: 1502741628 978

THE PERFECTING FAITH OF GOD'S SPA
Copyright ©2014 ALEDA J MARSHALL, All rights reserved.
ISBN-13: 978-1533577764 ISBN-10: 1533577765

TRACTS/BOOKLETS
HE AND ME FROM A TO Z
IS ANYONE OUT THERE?
ARE YOU READY FOR THE BATTLE?
WHAT DID YOU SAY?

DEDICATION

I dedicate this book to my mother, Jean Marshall. The chronicles of our journey together are inhabited with many considerations and contemplations. There have been challenging periods of uncertainty, inaccuracies and misjudgments sent to us from the gate of hell. However God, in His compassion and mercy saw fit to commission those seasons to further refine each of us into the image of His Son Jesus. Through such opportunities, He lovingly imparted to each of us His forgiveness, love, and strength as only He is able to do!

No matter what hellish falsehoods were bombarded at me to set me off course through the development of my lifespan to date, I was never abandoned by you or by God. Thank you mom for your love and for not abandoning me: at conception, in adolescence, in marriage, through divorce, through abandoning my children, being abandoned by my church, in abandoning myself or, through me being abandoned by my children.

You have loved me, and have been ever available to me; just a phone call away. Like the prodigal son's father, you have ever waited and watched, and with open arms, anticipated with celebration, the return of any of your brood's arrival home. You have taught me so much about God's strength, forgiveness, faithfulness, compassion and acceptance. Thank you for pointing me to God. We are Never Abandoned by Him. I love you.

ACKNOWLEDGMENTS

*¹¹ For I know the plans I have for you," declares the L*ORD*, "plans to prosper you and not to harm you, plans to give you hope and a future. ¹² Then you will call on me and come and pray to me, and I will listen to you. ¹³ You will seek me and find me when you seek me with all your heart.*
Jeremiah 29:11-13

TABLE OF CONTENTS

ABANDONED into ABUNDANCE

COPYRIGHTS	ii
ABOUT THE AUTHOR	iii
DEDICATION	v
ACKNOWLEDGMENTS	vi
TABLE OF CONTENTS	vii
INTRODUCTION	ix
1 ABANDONED AT CONCEPTION	1
2 ABANDONED IN ADOLESCENCE	10
3 ABANDONED IN MARRIAGE	21
4 ABANDONED IN DIVORCE	32
5 ABANDONED BY OUR CHURCH	43
6 ABANDONING OUR CHILDREN	54
7 ABANDONED BY ABORTION	67
8 ABANDONED BY SELF	78
9 ABANDONED BY OUR CHILDREN	89
CONCLUSION - NEVER ABANDONED BY GOD	100
WOULD YOU LIKE TO BE A CHILD OF GOD?	113

INTRODUCTION

> ... "LORD, there is no one like you to help the powerless against the mighty. Help us, LORD our God, for we rely on you ... LORD, you are our God; do not let mere mortals prevail against you." 2 Chronicles 14:11

Are we alone; abandoned by those most dear to us? Have we been conceived or did we conceive only to uncover that the consummator who had been the contributor in that conception, has **chosen** to vanish; **Abandoned at Conception**? Did we experience a trauma during our teen years that effected who and what we are today? Has or had our worlds shifted since, leaving our spirits stupefied as we stumble through our solitary scrambled feelings; forgotten and forlorn and **Abandoned in Adolescence**? Do we consider ourselves strangers in our relationship with our spouses; **Abandoned in Marriage**? Has a divorce caused us or, those whom are most dear to us, to thrown in the towel, walking off and walking out; leaving us **Abandoned in Divorce**? Is it possible that our church has deserted us in judgment; unloading us to succumb to our personal torments; **Abandoned by our Church**?

Maybe we are the ones who for any number of reasons have separated our lives from our children. Has that separation endangered the brittle emotions of each party, now left feeling disowned and discarded; **Abandoning our Children**? Perchance through some profound **choice** in our life, we may have mistakenly rendered an option that caused us to have **Abandoned by Abortion**? **Abandoned by Self** is not such an uncommon life style or condition these days. We do not hear the statistics daily, but the suicides related to those who are no longer able to carry their respective all-encompassing loads mount ever higher as time goes on. Are we there to offer someone a life vest in the midst of their storm? Maybe the pain of a divorce or any other number of factors has set adrift our children who now carry a burden of lack of forgiveness, bitterness, judgment, and rejection; disowning and renouncing us into a swamp of pity; **Abandoned by our Children**? We are forsaken; disregarded and discarded, incompatible and irrelevant, uninvited, and unwanted, and unwelcomed and useless.

Maybe we are the ones who have abandoned someone at some point in our lives. Is it possible that we are the ones who may be unwelcoming? Are we not going the extra mile to build a relationship with those God has preplanned and foreordained to cross our paths at a particular juncture; offering the clichéd proverbial *"cold shoulder"* instead? Have we made some poor *choices* in the past and are now at a loss as to how we may wash the slate clean? Are we sinking on our solo flight because we have abandoned a mate, our children, our parents, our church, or ourselves? Even though we may have repented and sought forgiveness, possibly the pain felt by those we may have injured, has cut so deep that it is currently impossible for them to yet forgive us. Do we want to put a pillow over our head in hopes that everything will work out just fine? Are we tired of the condemnation and desire to just run away and escape our current state of affairs? Have we done that before and that is why we are in our current predicament?

Or maybe we are wondering why the church we attend is not growing. Are we tearing down our personal walls, and in our own vulnerability, are we allowing the unwanted and forsaken to meet the smile, the eyes, the arms, and the heart of Jesus reflected through His Spirit residing within each of us? If not, maybe that is why there is no growth in our respective ministries. Is this **His will being done on earth as it is in heaven**?

> *and we know that in all things God works for the good of those who love him, who[a] have been called according to his purpose.* **Romans 8:28**

Yes, all things work together for good to them that love God, to those who are the called according to His purpose. However, maybe that promise is not currently visible in our present reality, or in our far-distant range? Even though we may have asked and received God's forgiveness, the wild oats that have been sown in our respective lives may take a bit of time to be completely weeded out of His Fruit of the Spirit garden that God tends in each of our hearts. Clearing the weeds and standing on the promises; is that not what faith is, believing in something that God has promised even though we may not presently see it (for the weeds)?

> *Now faith is confidence in what we hope for and assurance about what we do not see.* **Hebrews 11:1**

What have we been doing with the Word of God lately? Is it sitting on the table, in a bookcase, or perhaps, we do not have a clue as to where the "***BOOK***" might be? What does the gauge of our faith barometer "read in" at currently? Have we considered why we are here on this earth; what God's purpose might be for our respective lives? Or, do we consider ourselves too damaged; ***Abandoned by the world, God and self***? Let us embark on a journey of mercy, forgiveness, and washing the slate clean. Let us give and receive forgiveness, and with gratitude, rejoice on our personal adventures of renewal and restoration. Let us break free from the bondages of ***abandonment***, and become ***Abandoned in Abundance***; fulfilling our purpose, ***His will to be down on earth as it is in heaven***!

> ... because God has said, "Never will I leave you; never will I forsake you."[a] Hebrews 13:5

> ... And surely I am with you always, to the very end of the age. Matthew 28:20

1 ABANDONED AT CONCEPTION

> *[10] From birth I was cast on you; from my mother's womb You Have Been My God. [11] Do Not Be Far From Me, For Trouble Is Near And There Is No One To Help.* Psalm 22:10-11 (Emphasis supplied)

Were we **Abandoned at Conception**? As a consequence of a seed deposit by an earthly sperm donor, was our mother left alone to carry us; to reap this spur-of-the-moment harvest of fruit? Can anyone even identify the pollinator who by whatever form of coming together has now left us, the "little sprout" from within? In the plotting or maybe not so strategic planning for the joint union of our creation, had anyone considered the resulting ***abundance*** that possibly could be planted into our particular mother's tummy?

> *[15] My frame was not hidden from you when I was made in the secret place, when I was woven together in the depths of the earth. [16] Your eyes saw my unformed body; all the days ordained for me were written in your book before one of them came to be.* Psalm139:15-16

Possibly there was a decision to conceive and venture into a long-term relationship. Obviously, those life events may have changed drastically. There are always a few who ***choose*** not to maintain a committed combination. Whatever the scenario of our conception, our mothers became fertilized incubators. Each of them has endured that ninth month of pregnancy: lacking sleep, hardly able to physically arise up out of bed, or a chair for that matter; and they always had to pee! With or without expectations, our mothers may have imaginably or, unimaginably, been

Abandoned at Conception; left alone, with no form of mental, physical, emotional or financial support.

> *For you created my inmost being; you knit me together in my mother's womb.* **Psalm139:13**

Conceivably, no pun intended, we may be the unintended ***abundance*** of that coming together; ***Abandoned at Conception***. Were we birthed into a one parent home? Or, were we agonizingly or not so agonizingly surrendered by our birth parent(s)? Had we been adopted into a loving or maybe not so loving family? Whatever the circumstances of the many earthly reasons for our coming into being, we, as the offspring of such conception, will have most certainly pondered, and even probed over the years, the reasoning behind the reality of our respective being ***Abandoned at Conception***.

> *From birth I have relied on you; you brought me forth from my mother's womb. I will ever praise you.* **Psalm 71:6**

Maybe the term "***Abandonment***" is too harsh a term for many who may have been adopted into loving and somewhat well-functioning homes. Nevertheless, and more often than not, we, as the abandoned or surrendered "young ins", frequently speculate about the intricacies of that mysterious transferor of genetic material. The curiosity and conjure of our patented origin: "who we are", "do we look and act like them", may intermittently emerge from within our mind's "***imaginariums***" of possibilities.

Detecting at a very early age that others in our life's circle had a daddy in their reality, we may have contemplated or are still contemplating, where our daddy is. What does he look like? Where does he live? He certainly did not live with you and mom. If there are siblings in our families, we may come to recognize that we do not look like nor act like anyone in our home. In their denial of any semblance of similarity in appearance or disposition to where God has placed them, many biological children will often speculate and daydream about being adopted. They do not want to accept or even proclaim that they are kin to their particular and/or peculiar families. However, for those who believe that they were **Abandoned at Conception**, we surface to subconsciously suspect or, to at least discern, that we are odd in the realm of wherein we have been transplanted.

> *He is the Rock, his works are perfect, and all his ways are just. A faithful God who does no wrong, upright and just is he.* **Deuteronomy 32:4**

I guess one could say that I was born between "***a rock***" **and "*THE ROCK*"**. According to the Farmers' Almanac's Weather Time Machine that August 7TH day back in 1952, the temperature in St. Paul, Minnesota was to reach 83F with a dew point of 61F. Yes, I was brought forth into the humid Land of Lakes. Born a baby girl and weighing in at 7 lbs. 8 ½ ounces, this healthy little gift from God arrived at St. Joseph's Hospital at approximately 10:00 am, give or take a second or two. Sounds pretty normal so far, right? However, there was one thing missing; didn't it take two people to make me? Where was my dad?

Oh, my DAD, "***THE ROCK***", was ever present. He, after all is our Father God; and He, is "omnipresent". There would be no getting away from His surveillance and oversight. He will NEVER be absent from our goings on, for we, like all children He has created, are the "apple of His eye".

> [9] For ***The Lord's Portion Is His People ... His Inheritance.*** [10] *He found him in a desert land, and in the waste howling wilderness*; he led him about, he instructed him, ***He Kept Him As The Apple Of His Eye.*** [11] As an eagle stirreth up her nest, fluttereth over her young, spreadeth abroad her

wings, taketh them, beareth them on her wings: **¹² So The Lord Alone Did Lead Him …** Deuteronomy 32:9-12 KJV

Still, like others who believe they may have been **Abandoned at Conception**, there was a void in the roll call of my earthly dad, "**a rock**". Apparently, he was busy at the time, attending to other matters. You see, like countless other tales similar to this one, my earthly dad was married to someone else who was not my mom!

> *⁶ Is this the way you repay the LORD, you foolish and unwise people? Is he not your Father, your Creator,[a] who made you and formed you? ⁷ Remember the days of old; consider the generations long past. Ask your father and he will tell you, your elders, and they will explain to you.* **Deuteronomy 32:6-7**

Oh wait, I did not have an earthly father at the time of my birth or initial upbringing, to inquire about my family ancestry, as the above verse implies! Had he, like many other, not only been absent from our birth into this world, but even greater, *abandoned us at conception*? Had they forsaken God as they had forsaken us? Had they abandoned their "***ROCK***" of Salvation also? Did our earthly fathers forget the eternal FATHER that had formed them too?

> *¹⁵ … They abandoned the God who made them and rejected the Rock their Savior … ¹⁸ You deserted the Rock, who fathered you; you forgot the God who gave you birth.* **Deuteronomy 32:15b, 18**

Do we feel less than because we do not seem to fit into our environment? Are we often shouldering what we believe to be our lot in life; the liabilities imposed upon us: our circumstances, our disadvantages, our inhibitions, our limitations, etc.? Are we blaming the world and God because we were ***Abandoned at Conception***?

Remember Mary, the mother of Jesus? She became pregnant while she was engaged; only the child's father was not her fiancé Joseph. God sent an angel named Gabriel to Mary. Being a little alarmed first of all to be in the audience of an angel, Mary began to tremble even more so when the angel apprised her that she was to conceive a child. However, this child would not be the result of her union with her soon to be husband, Joseph. No; Gabriel told Mary that she was to be impregnated by the Holy Spirit with the Son of God.

> *[26] ... God sent the angel Gabriel ... [27] to a virgin pledged to be married to a man named Joseph ... The virgin's name was Mary. [28] The angel went to her and said, "Greetings, you who are highly favored! The Lord is with you ... [30] ... Do not be afraid, Mary; You Have Found Favor With God. [31] You Will Conceive And Give Birth To A Son, And You Are To Call Him Jesus ... [35] ... The Holy Spirit will come on you, and the power of the Most High will overshadow you. So the holy one to be born will be called[a] THE SON OF GOD."* Luke 1:26-28, 30-31, 35

Mary had been faithful to God. As a result of her commitment to Him, He highly favored her. The announcement of a child must have been rather shocking to Mary. She was a virgin. Mary had never ever been with a man. This would definitely take some explaining to her fiancé, family, relatives and neighbors! How was she going to break this news to Joseph? Would he believe that an angel had visited her? Who was going to imagine that such a purpose had been revealed for her life? She had not dreamed about this reality as a young girl.

Although Joseph was a little, or okay, maybe a lot, confounded and confused as Mary conveyed the events of the angel's visitation, and the anointed message professed, he still loved her. As a noble and just man, and not wanting to publically humiliate her, Joseph offered to divorce Mary quietly. What, we may ask; they are engaged, not married? The customs at the time, considered a couple already married at the point of the engagement; all except the living under the same roof and coming together as one. Those affairs would follow after the wedding feast.

> *Because Joseph her husband was faithful to the law, and yet[a] did not want to expose her to public disgrace, he had in mind to divorce her quietly.* **Matthew 1:19**

God always has things under control and never makes a mistake. All things are possible with God.

> **And he said, The *THINGS* which are impossible with men *Are Possible With God*. Luke 18:27 KJV**

After probably pondering all that Mary had related to him, and finally falling asleep that night, Joseph was also sent, by way of an angel and in the form of a dream, a specific message from God. In these many events, God had a purpose. Joseph and Mary had been elected to perform God's will as prophesized in days of old. The angel revealed to Joseph that Mary's conception and pregnancy was foreordained by God; conceived through the power of the Holy Spirit. The couple was to have a son. They were to name their new ***Abundance***, Jesus.

> [20] But while he thought on these things, behold, *the angel of the Lord appeared unto him in a dream,* saying, Joseph, thou son of David, *fear not to take unto thee Mary thy wife: for that which is conceived in her is of the Holy Ghost.* [21] *And she*

> *shall bring forth a son, and thou shalt Call His Name Jesus: for he shall save his people from their sins. [22]... which was spoken of the Lord by the prophet ... [23] Behold, a virgin shall be with child, and shall bring forth a son, and They Shall Call His Name Emmanuel ... GOD WITH US.* **Matthew 1:20-23 KJV**

As a man of God, elected for this purpose, Joseph obediently kept with the original wedding plans. However, he never had intercourse with Mary until after Jesus' birth.

> *[24] When Joseph woke up, he did what the angel of the Lord had commanded him and took Mary home as his wife. [25] But he did not consummate their marriage until she gave birth to a son. And he gave him the name Jesus.* **Matthew 1:24-25**

Does God's Word not say that He created us? Did not His eyes see our substance and knew that we would exist when there was yet none of us? When the rest of the world had no clue we would be arriving on their doorstep at some point in time, did God not know? Was not the pattern of our life and who we are, what we will look like, our hair color, the lengths of our toes, the shapes of our ears, our height and color of eyes, etc., already written in God's design book? Was that personalized blueprint not listed under our respective names? If someone has not told us this before, or maybe we just need a little reminding:

> *and we know that in all things God works for the good of those who love him, who[a] have been called according to his purpose.* **Romans 8:28**

Like Mary and Joseph, we have been created for a purpose. God has no limitations on the life He has pre-ordained for us. ***He Does Not Make Mistakes***! We have been designed to perform ***His will be done on earth as it is in heaven***. Have we accepted God's free gift of eternal life; a Salvation provided through the blood of Jesus shed at the cross? Has he washed away *ALL* of our sins? If not, please see *CHAPTER 12 WOULD YOU LIKE TO BE A CHILD OF GOD?*

If we have accepted Jesus as our Lord and our Savior, then when was the last time we recited the Lord's Prayer? When we accepted Jesus, welcoming Him into our hearts and lives, we became the anointed of God; *chosen* with a purpose. We have been set apart by God to fulfill His purpose here *on earth as it is in heaven*. What are the words of the Lord's Prayer: *"Thy kingdom come and Thy will be done on earth as it is in heaven"*? We have been *chosen* to make His will happen on earth as it is in heaven.

> *I can do all this through Him who gives me strength.* Philippians 4:13

As each of us by our lives, shines Who Christ is to the world wherever the frontiers of that expanse may range, we are, through our obedience, allowing the Light of God's heavenly kingdom to shine forth through us *"on earth as it is in heaven"*. He has promised that we can do *ALL THINGS* through Christ Who gives us the strength to accomplish His will. Let us ignore the lies from hell! We were not, are not, will be not, *Abandoned at Conception* by God.

We are fashioned for His purpose. As the anointed and appointed children of the most high God, we are to courageously reflect His love into a somewhat loveless world. His intended purpose for each of us is to: love, walk and fellowship with Him; to love, walk and fellowship with others; and to share the *abundance* of His love and will so that all may love and walk and fellowship with Him also. God does not make junk! We are the sum of many of His precious thoughts that are more in number than the sands of the earth. He is *always* with us.

> *¹⁷ How precious to me are your thoughts,[a] God! How vast is the sum of them! ¹⁸ Were I to count them, they would outnumber the grains of sand— when I awake, I am still with you.* Psalm139:17-18

Our Redeemer Jesus is continually praying and interceding on our behalf to our Father God; "**THE ROCK**". Let's face it; our Father God, or God Father, as affectionately referred to by my Pastor last Fathers' Day, is madly in love with us.

> *²⁷ And he who searches our hearts knows the mind of the Spirit, because the Spirit intercedes for God's people in accordance with the will of God .... ³⁴ Who then is the one who condemns? No one. Christ Jesus ... is at the right hand of God and is also interceding for us.* Romans 8:27, 34

> *... yea, I have loved thee with an everlasting love: therefore with loving kindness have I drawn thee.* Jeremiah 31:3 KJV

Will we **choose** to remain delusional about being **Abandoned at Conception** or, shall we **choose** to rise above? Shall we receive the fruit of being **chosen**; **Abandoned into Abundance** by our heavenly Father? God promises to never leave or forsake us. Jesus is on our side! He promises to be with each of us **ALWAYS**, even onto the end. **Never Abandoned by God**!

> *... because God has said, "Never will I leave you; never will I forsake you."*[a] Hebrews 13:5b

> *... And surely I am with you always, to the very end of the age.* Matthew 28:20b

2 ABANDONED IN ADOLESCENCE

> *... Be strong and courageous. Do not be afraid; do not be discouraged, for the LORD your God will be with you wherever you go."* **Joshua 1:9**

Were we **Abandoned in Adolescence**? Did our parents spend too much time at work? Maybe they separated or divorced, or possibly even one of them has been absent since our creation. Unfortunately, the remaining parent may have had to perform double duty to keep a roof over our head and food in our belly. As the whirlwind of bodily changes and hormone imbalances raged within our maturing beings, did we or do we find no one that we respect and trust who might be interested enough, has time enough and/or is willing enough to offer a listening ear? Are we **Abandoned in Adolescence**?

Maybe a traumatic event has crippled the family. Reasonably lost in a plausibly personalized despondency and/or attempting to rationalize the logic of it all, has each family member just shut down; withdrawing into self-sufficient directions within the confines of their confusion? Are we each just too baffled, bewildered, confused, damaged, hurt, and perplexed; forsaken and **Abandoned in Adolescence**? Determining that nobody understands us, or basically values who we are as human beings, do or did we establish that it would be much better for all those involved if we just launched out on our own? **Abandoning them in our adolescence**, do we too seek to escape by either physically or emotionally running away; or worse yet, taking our own life by suicide?

After my birth, mom and I resided in Minneapolis. A neighbor cared for me while mother worked as a nurse. However after sixteen months, we moved by train to

Canada wherein our family resided. Shortly thereafter, my mother was married. That nuptial gave me a dad, *"a rock"*, given to me by *"**THE ROCK**"*. Seeing pictures of us together at that time, leaves no doubt in my mind that I was his pride and joy. Father God had given me an earthly daddy! Bedecked in my little hat and white gloves, and proudly strutting my black patent shoes, whilst modeling my purse, my earthly father, mother and grandmother surrounded me with oodles of gratifying admiration, approval and attention. But there came a day when a new baby arrived; a baby they called, my brother.

That was fine in itself, but not long thereafter, another baby brother joined the fun. Even with Granny now residing with the family, my fondness quota was on a rapid decline, and dwindling fast. When it was announced that mother was to have her fourth baby, even Grandma moved out. Both mom and grandma had taught me to pray, and pray I did that this next baby would be a sister. I did not need any more brothers. As time pressed on, four more children were added to our one bathroom family home that supported four girls nesting in one bedroom and four boys bunked in another room. With both parents working and more children arriving, I found myself babysitting with greater frequency.

Seeking various captivations around the house wherein I might amuse myself, I soon discovered my parents personal, yet memory filled metal trunk in the basement of our abode. This exploration was one of my favorite treasures for the chest contained many mementos. There within the roughly three foot by two foot by two and one half foot tall container, I would idle away the hours; inspecting and admiring wedding pictures and other miscellaneous knick knacks. After many return occasions, I detected something on the wedding invitation that surprisingly, I had not noticed on my prior visits. That particular detail would be the date, specifically the year. The invite evidence their nuptial date as January 23, 1954. I knew their anniversary was on January 23, but had not given too much thought to the year. Wait a minute; was I not born on August 7, 1952? Should it not have been dated 1951 or at least, 1952? Was there an error on it?

Remember, my faculties did not absorb the circumstances of my first few years of life in order that I might be better able to make a fact based determination. Constructed on the details of which I was now mindful, I concluded that I perhaps had been born before they were married. I had been exposed to or overheard conversations regarding other people whose life events had transpired in that pattern. And yet, I never tackled the topic to clarify those specifics at that time with my mother. I certainly never deemed that my earthly dad, "**the rock**", was not my biological father.

Sometimes referred to by the younger generation of our family as "little grandma", my mom's mom was often my respite in the tumultuous storms frequently flaring in large families. However, sometimes I would spend the weekend visiting with my paternal grandparents; you know, "**the rock**'s" mom and dad. On this particular weekend, my parents and the rest of the brood must have taken a trip. Possibly, for my own sanity, I was cleared to remain behind and join my paternal grandparents for the weekend. My father's youngest brother still lived at home with my grandparents. On this particular weekend stay, my uncle had his girlfriend visiting. We were conversing about the various irregularities in the overall lives of his eight older and married brothers and sisters; my aunts and uncles.

However, at one point, the dialogue took a rather bizarre twist. Whilst listening to a topic that for me at the time had the divergence of entering the twilight zone, my ears soon became flooded with information that confounded me to my core. Being pleasingly agreeable and nodding to whatever inquiry was being presented to me, I purposefully attempted to maintain somewhat of an indifferent to compliant poker face. I do not remember where my grandparents were during this conversation. Questions or statements similar to, "you know your dad is not your biological father, don't you?" "Oh ya! I knew that", I responded, attempting to masquerade my stunned self. My uncle continued with comparisons to other members of the extended family's situations. However, in the shock and awe of what my young adolescent brain was straining to sort, I wanted to go home and straighten out this confusion.

Upon my families return from their travels the next day, my father picked me up at my grandparents, and we departed for home. I do not recall my exact mindset, events and activities that followed as they transpired. My guess is that I quickly sat in the back seat of the car, quietly stifling the tears streaming down my face on the ride home. All that I could think about in the uprising of my surmounting emotions was the fact that this man driving the car was not my biological father. When I walked through the doors of the family home that day, I immediately retreated to my bedroom in sobs. I say my bedroom because, in their wisdom, my parents had sensed and supported from a very early age that space and quiet time for pondering and studying would be a life's essential for me. However, being granted my privacy, denied my sisters entry until bed time.

Witnessing my emotional behavior over the next few days, mother sensed that something was not right. She had no idea what was going on, and I did not have the courage to approach her with the topic. Considering the memories of my many contemplations and occurrences that arose over the days that followed, I recall imagining and assuming any number of scenarios. As chief cook and bottle washer, there was going to be mutiny on the bounty when my brothers and sisters found out that I was not really their big bossy sister. They will never follow my directions again when in my care. There is no doubt in my mind that they will tar and feather me. Sometimes referred to as "queenie", I suspected that this would be the end of my reign! Other thoughts plagued me as well. Specifically, my contemplations probed the fact that I felt as though I was not really part of this family any longer. I was never really like this tribe of misfits anyway! Did I not have blond hair? Who am I; had I been ***Abandoned in Adolescence***?

During my "little grandma's" visit in the course of that next week, I had no distress in ambushing and flabbergasting her with the exposé and the many questions associated with such. I felt abandoned, deceived, isolated, out of control, out of place, shocked, and terrified; I think you get my point. As I said earlier, Granny had become somewhat of a confident to me in my maturing. With such a large family, the home continually needed to be cleaned and tidied. Granny was often found fussing about with such things. Setting my trap, I slithered into the kitchen and sat down at the kitchen table. The poor little old lady standing at the kitchen sink washing dishes had no idea what was to transpire.

Casually broaching the topic, I commenced my inquiry as to why mother had never told me that my dad, "*a rock*", was not my biological father. Well the petite five foot tall thing who could be scared half to death at the drop of a hat, nearly crumbled beneath her weakening knees. She was probably 65 or 66 years of age at the time. She no longer babysat our family as she felt that we were much too unruly and mischievous. Observing her trying to maintain her composure whilst clinging to the kitchen sink in an attempt to remain vertical, Granny first queried me as to wherein I had heard what I was professing. She was probably stalling for time to respond. And then the excuses and humming and hawing began, "You are such a sensitive child"; "no one knew how you would take the truth". I really don't remember much else as I then slithered back out of the kitchen, continuing to ruminate on this upheaval.

Shortly thereafter, mother was dressing one of the children on the dinner table; again in the kitchen, and obviously a focal point of our family home. As I entered and quietly sat down, she calmly repeated the same sputtering reasoning about sensitivity that Granny had uttered to me several days before. I felt as though I no longer belonged in this home. In my mind at the time, this man was not my "real" father. These kids were not my "real" brothers and sisters. I felt betrayed and **Abandoned in Adolescence**! My life was over with no place to escape.

Do we recall that Joseph was not Jesus' biological father either? In Luke 2 of the New Testament, we learn of Jesus' earthly family's annual travel to Jerusalem for the Feast of Passover. At the conclusion of the feast, always compliant Jesus, was nowhere to be found. Mary and Joseph assumed that He was travelling on ahead with the retreating relatives or other families from their town. Believing such, Mary and Joseph also launched on their trek home. Realizing after their one day's journey that Jesus was not with the returning group, they retraced their steps; eventually returning to Jerusalem.

After a frantic hunt, they uncovered Jesus in the Temple, seated among the teachers. He was listening to and asking questions of them. The teachers were amazed at His wisdom. Jesus' life was not to be like others in His family. As a teenager, Jesus was aware of His Father God's plans for His life; His divine purpose. At the Temple, Jesus was seeking the Oneness with His heavenly Father. Jesus was not the son of Joseph, but rather, the Son of God. Jesus was created for a divine purpose and He was preparing to be about His Father's business in that purpose, here on earth.

> ... *"Why were you searching for me?" he asked. "Didn't you know I had to be in my Father's house?"[a]* **Luke 2:49**

On seeing His parents and hearing their query, Jesus responds to them with His own question and statement of fact: "why are you looking for Me; didn't you realize that I must be about my Father's business?" His mortal parents did not grasp the meaning of His words and the day's events. However, Mary never forgets them. Returning home, she pondered them deep within her mind; recalling the angel's announcement at His conception.

> *⁵⁰ But they did not understand what he was saying to them. ⁵¹ Then he went down to Nazareth with them and was obedient to them. But his mother treasured all these things in her heart.* **Luke 2:50-51**

Mary, Joseph, and Jesus each were born unto this earth to fulfill our heavenly Father's purpose. The purpose God has for each of our lives may not fit into the status quo of those around us. By what we might consider to be life's disadvantages, God intends to direct to strengthen and to equip us to be better suited to care for others on this earth. His desire is for us to express to others the ***abundance*** of the love that we have received from Him. As we display His love, His purpose ***will be done on earth as it is in heaven*** through us to those on our earthly sojourn.

Jacob, whom later God renamed Israel, had twelve sons. One of his youngest sons was named Joseph. He was prized by his father. Openly expressing that favor, his father had a custom designed multicolored coat made specifically for Joseph. His brothers were extremely jealous of him. In addition, Joseph was quite the dreamer. One day Joseph recounted a particularly perplexing dream to his father and brothers. Upon hearing it, his brothers hated him even more for what his dream implied.

> *⁷ We were binding sheaves of grain out in the field when suddenly my sheaf rose and stood upright, while your sheaves gathered around mine and bowed down to it." ⁸ His brothers said to him, "Do you intend to reign over us? Will you actually rule us?" And they hated him all the more because of his dream and what he had said.* **Genesis 37:7-8**

Although Joseph was an adolescent and possibly did not completely understand his dream, God was beginning to reveal His purpose for Joseph's life. Having yet another dream, the stage had been set for Joseph to launch on his mysterious journey to fulfill God's purpose.

> *⁹ ... he had another dream, and he told it to his brothers. "Listen," he said, "I had another dream, and this time the sun and moon and eleven stars were bowing down to me." ¹⁰ When he told his father as well as his brothers, his father rebuked him and said, "What is this dream you had? Will your mother and I and your brothers actually come and bow down to the ground before you?"* **Genesis 37:9-10**

In their jealous, Joseph's brothers now planned to kill him. After much debate, it was agreed that they would not slay him but rather sell him to travelling traders passing by on camels. Having soaked his multicolored coat in sheep's blood, the brothers returned it to their father as evidence of Joseph's death. And we think our lives are "topsy-turvy". As a teenager, Joseph was sold as a slave, taken from his family, his land, and sent into another country;

Abandoned in Adolescence. Why we might ask; because God had a purpose for his life that could only be accomplished in this fashion. Remember:

> *and we know that in all things God works for the good of those who love him, who[a] have been called according to his purpose.* **Romans 8:28**

Joseph prospered initially in Egypt, finding favor with his master, but then he was falsely accused and sent to prison. In his various jailhouse experiences, God was using His Word that Joseph's father had taught him to prepare Joseph for the job he was to do for Him. Joseph had to ***choose*** what he was going to reflect on in his mind during his prison terms. What was he going to contemplate during all those long days of confinement? I am sure he was wondering how many more days he would remain there; falsely accused. Being left behind and forgotten, ***Abandoned in Adolescence*** and now a man, Joseph finally got the message and accepted the ***truth***. He remembered the ***truth*** his father taught him as a young boy. That ***truth*** would finally set him ***free***!

> *And ye shall know the truth, and the truth shall make you free.* **John 8:32 KJV**

God had a divinely appointed purpose for Joseph's life. He found favor in the eyes of God. In addition Joseph was respected by Pharaoh whom he ultimately worked for in preparations for one of the greatest famines in history. Joseph became Pharaoh's right hand man. His dreams and interpretation thereof revealed a great famine was to come. Joseph assisted Pharaoh in preparing for it in the land of Egypt. In the end, this divine arrangement saved Joseph's family from dying of lack due to the famine in their land. What his brothers meant for Joseph's harm, God intended for good to save people's lives.

> *But God sent me ahead of you to preserve for you a remnant on earth and to save your lives by a great deliverance.[a]*. Genesis 45:7
>
> *[19] But Joseph said to them, "Don't be afraid. Am I in the place of God? [20] You intended to harm me, but God intended it for good to accomplish what is now being done, the saving of many lives.* Genesis 50:19-20

From the time I was a child, I believed Father God, "***THE ROCK***", had His hand on my life; I had a purpose. Even after accepting Jesus as my Savior, it still took me many years to grasp that God had an anointed and appointed purpose for me. That is why He creates each of us. Again, let us be reminded, we are here as His representatives to facilitate ***His will to be done on earth as it is in heaven***. How?

> ... With men this is impossible; <u>but</u> *WITH GOD ALL THINGS ARE POSSIBLE.* Matthew 19:26 KJV

Life is often confusing in adolescence, and even more so when one discovers they are adopted or bears a life changing event such as divorce or a death, or even under the norm. ***But for GOD***; He is in control. He desires to build His character in each of us; a character that is to be a reflection of Him; His love and ***His will be done on earth as it is in heaven***. However, like Joseph, a vast number of broken people with ever changing life's circumstances are evolving in this world. Through the handiwork of God, the Master craftsman, we are being molded and empowered through our specific sets of circumstances; designed to chisel us into His ***abundance***. We are the Chosen, ***Abandoned into Abundance***, to go and bring forth fruit.

> Ye have not chosen me, but *I HAVE CHOSEN YOU, and ORDAINED YOU*, that ye should *GO*

> *AND BRING FORTH FRUIT*, and that your fruit should remain ... John 15:16 KJV

By our *choosing* to escape the lies of hell, designed by the enemy himself to hinder and destroy each of us, and by our *choosing* to turn our *Abandonment into Abundance*, we obediently fulfill His purpose in leading others on the way to Him; to become *NEW* also. What did Jesus say?

> *... I am the way, the truth, and the life: no man cometh unto the Father, but by Me.* John 14:6 KJV

> *... if any man be in Christ, he is a NEW creature: old things are passed away; behold, ALL THINGS ARE BECOME NEW.* 2 Corinthians 5:17 KJV

Forgetting what is behind, what had to be broken to get us to this point, we become *NEW*! We press on!

> [12] *not that I have already attained*, or am already perfected; *BUT I PRESS ON* ... [13] ... *I do not count myself to have apprehended; but one thing I do, Forgetting Those Things Which Are Behind And Reaching Forward To Those Things Which Are Ahead,* [14] *I Press Toward The Goal* for the prize of the upward call of God in *Christ Jesus.* Philippians 3:12-14 KJV

What will we *choose*; *Abandoned into Abundance* or to remain *Abandoned in Adolescence*? God is bigger than our little world or our pity party. We were never *Abandoned in Adolescence; Never Abandoned by God!*

> *... because God has said, "Never will I leave you; never will I forsake you."*[a] Hebrews 13:5b

> *... And surely I am with you always, to the very end of the age.* Matthew 28:20b

3 ABANDONED IN MARRIAGE

> ... *'Not by might nor by power, but by my Spirit,'*
> *says the* LORD *Almighty.* **Zechariah 4:6 KJV**

Are we beginning to perceive that we have been **Abandoned in Marriage**? Has a glacier fragment drifted into our sanctimonious wedding beds, wedging itself fixed center between us and our mates in our frigid bedsteads? Do we inquire as to whom the strange bedfellow is who rolls away from us each night, giving us the cold shoulder?

After I graduated from a Catholic girl's school in Canada and launched into the hippy-dippy anti-war culture of the early 70's, I spiritually closed the door on God. My Christian upbringing would prevent me from outrageously skipping my way into the flower child free love period of that present age. That spiritual conscience would modestly awaken again through pre-marital counseling and my wedding vows. However, the critical motivation transpired after the birth of our first child when I questionably began grasping that I might be **Abandoned in Marriage**.

With an insatiable appetite to achieve all that the world had to offer, I notched off another triumph when I relocated to the USA. Recently returning from a sojourn in Europe, my hometown in Canada no longer maintained the same draw. A Canadian friend's contact uncovered a place for me to dwell just off the University of Minnesota's West Bank campus in Minneapolis. It was a diverse tenement with multifarious efficiencies and one room units that required the sharing of community kitchens and bathrooms. It was in that tenement wherein I met my soon to be husband.

Apparently through the course of observing my many dashes to safety whilst avoiding the dart match driven hallway missiles, he had settled his nuptial objective. Yes, he would just have to get to know me, his future bride. Through the various tenant group interactions, I never surely recognized that he was even interested in me. He was extremely introspective, loved gadgets and watching TV; specifically Star Trek and Kung Fu. Running out of money between jobs and fancying to stay in the country a little while longer, I exchanged my more expensive all inclusive efficiency apartment for my future husband's low-cost, one room, facility sharing module. Also, I offered to clean his abode, prepare his meals, and wash his dishes and his laundry, in exchange for food.

Not sure of the direction of this vague relationship, and needing to make some responsible **choices**, I elected to move back to Canada. As I settled in, acquiring a decent job and establishing a residence, I began receiving numerous candid letters from what I thought to be, one very detached individual; you know, the dart throwing neighbor. One evening after now one of our many lengthy phone calls, he concluded with: "the sink is full of dishes and all my clothes are dirty". After hanging up the phone, I pondered as to whether that might have been a marriage proposal.

He spoke intelligently, when you could get him to talk. Somehow managing to avoid being drafted into the military, he had graduated college with a double major in Art and Philosophy. When I met his family, they displayed civility, finesse, and refinement. He was an only child of controlling older parents whose dialogues developed primarily around congenialities. Based on my revised mate selection criteria, he was perfect; the exact opposite of me! Our families were different in many ways, too. His family style was unemotional and diplomatic; my family was noisy and verbose. I was the oldest of eight with younger parents; he was an only child of older, more mature parents. His family had a trust fund; I had a family to trust.

Moreover, he was a college grad. I had aspirations of college as a high school grad. Our religions were very similar and yet different. He was raised Lutheran and I was raised Catholic. However, who knew what belief we would have together with his philosophy opinions in our hippy genera. Many say that Canada is very similar to the USA. That fact is true, but there are many cultural differences. My enamor was captivated by not only the novelty of this new country, but with this man who had already achieved so much of what I had yet not attained. After a subsequent phone call to clarify the fact that there was indeed a proposal, my groom-to-be soon materialized in Canada.

Following the request and subsequent approval by my dad, "**the rock**" for my hand in marriage, I was transported back across the border to be wedded happily ever after. Not! How was it possible for me to believe that he truly wanted to marry someone such as myself? What was I bringing to the table? I retained such inflated high esteem and respect for this man's birthright; comparing all that he could tender in relation to all that I was not? Was that love? I was not able to make a Godly *choice*. What did I know about love? As time elapsed on this not so fairy tale journey, the blacken tarnish began to emerge on my great knight's armor. Sin reared its ugly head in our wedded bliss' nightmare and I felt **Abandoned in Marriage**.

Even though each of our elementary religious guidance provided us a form of spiritual groundwork from our respective churches, it was the somber urgency of the certainty of our then current life's critical circumstances that finally crushed what remaining self-sustaining support we, in our respective pride and stubbornness, had clung. Our first year of marriage drove us into marriage counseling. These culminating forces finally caused each of us to fall kneeling at the foot of the cross, SINNERS, and yet, total strangers; **Abandoned in Marriage**.

> **But God commendeth His love toward us, in that, while we were yet sinners, Christ died for us. Romans 5:8 KJV**

We were polar opposites, except for the fact that we were both strong willed and determined; unyielding to "the two shall become one flesh" decree. His silent introspections would often set off my verbose rants. Then, feeling ***Abandoned in Marriage***, I would ventilate, questioning as to whether the walls, the doors or even the windows might be listening to me, for he certainly appeared to not be. I alleged that I was ***Abandoned in Marriage***. We had just become parents to a baby girl. Realizing by her birth and the facts at hand, we comprehended that we both had been on a spiritual detour for a long time; we had lost our way. We required direction, but first we needed forgiveness.

> *If we confess our sins, He is faithful and just to forgive us our sins, and to cleanse us from all unrighteousness.* 1 John 1:9 KJV

> *JESUS SAITH unto him, I am the way, the truth, and the life: no man cometh unto the Father, but by Me.* John 14:6 KJV

The blessing of those harsh inevitabilities assisted us in realizing that we were sinners. The germinated seed of our marriage wherein "the two shall become one flesh" was dying because of our rapidly increasing respective mounds of lack of forgiveness. We could no longer stay together in our own strength; in this cesspool of bitterness and resentment. Were we both ***Abandoned in Marriage***? Compelled to tear down the walls surrounding each of our individual heart's current abodes would require the best instruments in our respective tool belts to properly construct this new wedded house. We sought God's mercy through His forgiveness. Receiving that forgiveness, we committed ourselves to Him.

> *For God so loved the world that he gave his one and only Son, that whoever believes in him shall not perish but have eternal life.* **John 3:16**
>
> *If you declare with your mouth, "Jesus is Lord," and believe in your heart that God raised him from the dead, you will be saved.* **Romans 10:9**

Had I entered into this relationship for all the wrong reasons? I did not even know who I was; never mind if I could truly love my husband or others, including myself. I didn't even know if I liked myself! I was trying to live through this man's world of experiences; what he had already received or what he had already realized; all aspirations that I had not yet achieved personally. My self-esteem was wrapped up in him; and he did not even seem to enjoy talking to me, being my friend or physically expressing his love to me. What was wrong with me? I detected that I was so alone; ***Abandoned in Marriage***.

Learning how to receive forgiveness would help me to understand how to forgive and how to love; understanding how to forgive myself, and then finally ascertaining how to forgive others. As I have already described, God had already expressed His love to me through His mercy released through Jesus' death on the cross.

> *And so we know and rely on the love God has for us. God is love. Whoever lives in love lives in God, and God in them.* **1 John 4:16**

God provided me with many resources to advance my spiritual journey. Through our local country community church, its members, Christian radio and various other sources of Christian seminars, Bible studies and fellowship, as well as what He re-enforced during my personal prayer times and Bible lessons, God began to plant the seeds of His Fruit of the Spirit within my heart. As with all of our lives, my route has met with a number of perplexing trials and detours to this stage. Hence, I have to admit that the road to understanding love has been a long expedition.

> *[4] Love is patient, love is kind. It does not envy, it does not boast, it is not proud. [5] It does not dishonor others, it is not self-seeking, it is not easily angered, it keeps no record of wrongs. [6] Love does not delight in evil but rejoices with the truth. [7] It always protects, always trusts, always hopes, always perseveres. [8] Love never fails ... [13] And now these three remain: faith, hope and love. But the greatest of these is love.* **1 Corinthians 13:4-8a, 13**

Now married two and one half years, my behavior did not demonstrated any of these attributes. I was 24 years old and I had just delivered our first child. We were attempting to build a house on 16 raw wooded acres in the country. Our home in town had sold four times before a closing deal finalized. I was not feeling any love except for the miracle of our baby. Anything that could go wrong went wrong, and I blamed everything on my husband.

> *Greater love hath no man than this, that a man lay down his life for his friends.* **John 15:13 KJV**

How was I to lay down my life for a man that minimally conversed with me? The desperate and insecure thoughts present in our expedited premarital courtship now questioned my spiritual walk. However, through His Word, God would ease my fears as He soothingly whispered to me:

> *... if any man be in Christ, he is a new creature: old things are passed away; behold, ALL THINGS ARE BECOME NEW.* **2 Corinthians 5:17 KJV**

As a new person in Christ, I purposed to love my husband and God with all my heart and soul, and with all my mind and strength. However, it was readily apparent to both of them that I was still weak. My heart wrenching pride, current lack of respect for and condescending attitude displayed towards my husband was not the love harvest God desired to reap from this Fruit of the Spirit garden that He had been cultivating in my heart. No matter how much counseling or varying therapists we sought help from, or how much I memorized all those submission Scriptures, or how many Christian marriage seminars we attended, we did not have much of an interpersonal relationship. I was **Abandoned in Marriage**.

In spite of me desperately trying to learn how to be the perfect submissive Christian wife, this man, in this separate secluded existences of our relationship was driving me crazy. How could I love like God? No one has ever loved and cared for me like Him. With the birth of a son several years later, it was becoming readily apparent that a new sprout of communication and love was blooming as observed in my husband's rapport with our young children. He was a marvelously wonderful "daddy", as well as an exceptional play pal. Why did he not try to have a fraction of that relationship with me? Why was I **Abandoned in Marriage**?

> *... Yea, I have loved thee with an everlasting love: therefore with lovingkindness have I drawn thee.*
> **Jeremiah 31:3 KJV**

My expression of God's love commanded that I not love the world. Being of the world, I am, however duty-bound to love my husband; my family; the church; and any and all those that berate me, bear false witness about me through defamation, denigration and disparagement. These words probably sound easier expressed on paper than in actual reality. That is in fact true. However, didn't Jesus' accuser do the same to Him as He prepared to offer Himself as a ransom for all of our sins on the cross He was to hang?

As the years progressed, I would oftentimes ponder with burning envy, as I observed other married couples savoring in each other's company together. Analyzing and dissecting each move of their hands and bodies as they lovingly held hands, cherishingly stole tender kisses or imparted an adoring caress or hug, I would wonder why I did not have that type of relationship with my husband. From the commencement of our relationship, we rarely, if ever shared such cherished moments. What was wrong with me? Had I been **Abandoned in Marriage**?

Due to some pre-martial encounters, I was not always convinced of the undivided devotion of my salesman husband's heart. Maybe my insecurities were still simmering forth from our brief pre-marital encounters and affairs that had transpired during that period. My folks were very physically expressive. Possibly because my husband's father was a remarried widower and his parents were older, he had never been exposed to such as an example. Were they too each **Abandoned in Marriage**?

I cannot speak for my husband but in my determination to succeed in having a Godly marriage, I still repeatedly sensed that I was just coexisting with him; oftentimes feeling completely hollow inside. Had lack of courtship and diverse foundational realities, left me feeling alone, void of the "two shall become one flesh" anointing of our marriage? The relational truth of this potential reality was already crushing my clenched, crestfallen heart, constricting within my chest. I was desperate and depressed. Was I **Abandoned in Marriage**?

In the thirteen years of our marriage, I had been confronted with heartache and have wept many tears due to dejection, despair and downheartedness. Many endure this same pain in their respective marriages. I desperately wanted my husband to love me. Conversely, this same lack of affection drove me further into the arms of Jesus. I entreated Him for an outpouring of His joy that I knew only He could provide. Jesus loves us with an everlasting love. As Christians, we are the Bride of Christ. As His Bride, we will never be *Abandoned in Marriage*.

> **FOR THY MAKER IS THINE HUSBAND; the Lord of hosts is His name; and thy Redeemer the Holy One of Israel; The God of the whole earth shall He be called. Isaiah 54:5 KJV**

I know there may be others out there who may feel *Abandoned in Marriage*. However, Jesus is our Light in the darkness and our Anchor in the storm. Whether we obediently *choose* to stay in our marriages or leave for whatever reason may be determined at the time, nobody has promise to be with us like God.

> *When Jesus spoke again to the people, he said, "I am the light of the world. Whoever follows me will never walk in darkness, but will have the light of life."* **John 8:12**

> *We have this hope as an anchor for the soul, firm and secure* ... **Hebrews 6:19**

As God's Word evidences, we are here to perform His will; *His will to be done on earth as it is in heaven*; His will and His purpose. We are to be His sweet fragrance of His victory over death and eternal damnation to those who may know Jesus and to those who without Him will perish through eternal death.

> *[14] But thanks be to God, who always leads us as captives in Christ's triumphal procession and uses us to spread the aroma of the knowledge of him everywhere. [15] For we are to God the pleasing aroma of Christ among those who are being saved and those who are perishing. [16] To the one we are an aroma that brings death; to the other, an aroma that brings life. And who is equal to such a task?* **2 Corinthians 2:14-16**

Our God's love is able to teach us to forgive and love our husbands, our children, and our neighbors, just as He is teaching us to love ourselves. And still if those around us continue to be unlovable, like some of those who are not even our enemies, then all the more so, we are to forgive and love them anyway with His agape love. We can only accomplish this with God's grace. This will be a lifelong tutorial; a thorn in the flesh that may be readily challenged at every turn by the gates of hell. We are not required to be a particular individual's best friend, but we are required to love and pray for the sinner. We are to hate the sin only!

> **And the second is like unto it, Thou shalt *LOVE THY NEIGHBOUR AS THYSELF*. Matthew 22:39 KJV**

> **But I say unto you, *love your enemies, bless them that curse you, do good to them that hate you, and pray for them which despitefully use you, and persecute you*; Matthew 5:44 KJV**

At this juncture, I continue to seek God's loving forbearance and mercy. We may not know how to love our husband, our neighbor, or anyone else with this kind of agape love that we may still not yet understand. However, we can still ascertain how to forgive and love others; including our respective selves. I do know that we can expect Jesus, our Groom, to hold our hands and walk with each of us, His

Bride, in the ***abundance*** of His eternal love. He will direct us by His Spirit. He will never ***Abandoned in Marriage***!

Do we sense that we have been ***Abandoned in Marriage***? Are we losing the desire to be married to our mates? Through sin, people will disappoint and hurt us. However, our God, in His ever loving woos on the quest of the ***abundance*** of His eternal love affair, will teach each of us how to love no matter the state of our earthly wed. We are the Bride of Christ, and Jesus is our Groom. The more we allow Him to heal us through His Word, the more we are able to forgive and to love. Through the healing balm of His Word, God whispers that He knows us, and has known us from the beginning of time. He has made us. And through the same Word, Jesus discloses to us that before we knew Him, before we committed our respective lives to Him, He has loved each of us, His Bride, with His everlasting love.

Do we desire to be ***Abandoned into Abundance*** or to remain ***Abandoned in Marriage***? Are we expressing His love and shining His Light in accomplishing ***His will to be done on earth as it is in heaven***? Jesus is always available to comfort us, to listen to us, to embrace us, to love us, and to guide us. He will never leave us or forsake us. His Bride will never be ***Abandoned in Marriage***.

> *... because God has said, "Never will I leave you; never will I forsake you."*[a] **Hebrews 13:5b**
>
> *... And surely I am with you always, to the very end of the age.* **Matthew 28:20b**

4 ABANDONED IN DIVORCE

> *Be strong and of a good courage, fear not, nor be afraid of them: for the Lord thy God, He it is that doth go with thee*; **HE WILL NOT FAIL THEE, NOR FORSAKE THEE.** Deuteronomy 31:6 KJV

Perhaps that iceberg refuses to thaw and one of us in our frustration has raised the topic of divorce! Are we astonished, bewildered and confounded, blaming God for our mess? Have we sought our Maker, only to be rejected by this marriage breaker; **Abandoned in Divorce**? Obedience hurts sometimes, especially when we are encamped about by the disparaging foul smells often associated with divorce. There are no air fresheners strong enough to conceal the stench of hatred, bitterness, regret, judgment, condemnation and lack of forgiveness, emitted therein.

As I shared in the previous chapter titled, **ABANDONED IN MARRIAGE**, I have been tested with heartache and have wept many tears due to the emotional and physical denial in my marriage. My jealousy would often simmer as I observed other couples; many appearing to truly enjoy each other's harmony together. Why did we not have that type of relationship? I do not recall us ever truly relating in that fashion. Now, I was to be **Abandoned in Divorce**.

After many years of various Christian marriage counseling, seminars and the like, my husband finally admitted to one of our last analysts that by not talking to me or having personal relations with me, he believed that he was attaining some form of control in our relationship. We were great business partners and managed our household and ministry service without a flaw. No one was ever aware that there were problems in the perfectionist picture of our nuptial bliss, except for some close confidents of mine. I had to talk to someone! Was I ***Abandoned in Divorce***?

In addition, and as I also imparted in the previous chapter, due to some pre-martial encounters, I was not always convinced of the undivided devotion of the salesman's heart residing within my husband. Maybe my earlier insecurities were still simmering forth. To my knowledge, my husband was always faithful, but was he? The relational truth of this potential reality was already crushing my clenched, crestfallen heart, constricting within my chest. I was desperate, depressed and so lonely. The rest of the world seems to be attracted to me; why was my husband not? Considered by some fairly attractive, I was tall, thin (more so at the time) and had long blondish hair that hung nearby my waist. It was not uncommon when servicing our home or at the home repair shop or, maybe even walking the neighborhood, to catch a roving glance in my direction, or hear remarks or, a whistle, in my husband's absence.

From time to time, we may hear sermons requiring woman to render or offer their bodies to their husbands, but we rarely hear any homilies on the reverse application as is also provided for in the Word. The reason God commands this is so that we do not fall into sin. As I desperately clung to the hem of Jesus' robe, seeking wisdom throughout all these years of being ***Abandoned in Marriage***, I pondered where my protection was. Aware of the exact days of both of our children's conceptions might be a significant clue as to the incidence of our personal relations. God was supposed to be bigger than this and able to fix it. He had not, and I was enraged; now being ***Abandoned in Divorce***.

> *[3] The husband should fulfill his marital duty to his wife, and likewise the wife to her husband. [4] The wife does not have authority over her own body but yields it to her husband. In the same way,*

> *the husband does not have authority over his own body but yields it to his wife. ⁵Do not deprive each other except perhaps by mutual consent and for a time, so that you may devote yourselves to prayer. Then come together again so that Satan will not tempt you because of your lack of self-control.* 1 Corinthians 7:3-5

And so as the years progressed, we continued to strive in our marriage. The blessing of that effort stimulated me to seek the presence of God for strength and wisdom in becoming not only my husband's submissive bride, but my Groom Jesus' submissive Bride. I had watched my mother struggle herself through some very challenging periods with my earthly father, "***a rock***". I knew that I would never have had the strength to overcome such trials. In my family, divorce was not an option. Now, I was being taught to trust God, and not leaning on my own understanding. I was being broken. I am eternally grateful for these lessons learned during these quiet, and not so quiet trials of clinging to the hem of Jesus' garment.

> *"... I say these things while I am still in the world, so that they may have the full measure of my joy within them.* John 17:13

Many endure this same pain in their respective marriages. I entreated God for an outpouring of His joy; a joy that could only be provided by Him. I always had Him. He loved me with an everlasting love! After all, is He not our Strength, our Hope, our Deliverer, our Provider, our Healer, our Restorer; our "**ROCK**"? Is He not the Lord God Almighty? Is He not able to do over and above our greatest expectations, hopes, dreams, and desires?

> *Now to him who is able to do immeasurably more than all we ask or imagine, according to his power that is at work within us,* Ephesians 3:20

However, were all those efforts void as we divorced rather abruptly after 13 years of marriage? My heart was shattered when I witness, unbeknownst to my husband, a very conceding circumstance. I am not a prude, however, the reality of the emotional toll of the bondage associated with his abandonment and control finally became the straw that broke the camel's back. Why did he not want to have an interpersonal or intimate relationship with me? I was no longer going to be ignored; unloved by someone who throughout our thirteen years of marriage still ***chose*** to express a bizarre form of controlled relationship. There was maybe some deep seeded reason for that in retrospect, but I am explaining how I was feeling at the time. It was now "me, me, me". I was alone; ***Abandoned in Marriage*** long enough. If he didn't want me, then someone else would!

I had vowed and endeavored to continue trusting God in this relationship. However, I now found myself rejected and devastated by what I had witnessed. This marriage was no longer the fruit of my commitment and labor expended. Becoming not only angry with my husband but very outraged at God as well, I slammed my spiritual door shut tight. I admittedly entered into rebellion. Is this the reward for believing and being so committed to this marriage and my family; ***Abandoned in Divorce***? As I said earlier, no one but a few ever knew we had any problems.

In my rebellion that followed, my reality of so many aspects that I believed to be foundational to life came tumbling down. In my confusion and inability to disclose or understand the root cause of the reality of our issues, I maintained my rebellious front. It has taken many years to heal from the breaking of these events. In that time, our faithful God has imparted to me through His Word that He too has wept over the rebellion of His children.

> ³ but *thou hast played the harlot with many lovers; yet return again to Me*, saith the Lord... ²⁰ Surely *as a wife treacherously departeth from her husband*, so have *Ye Dealt Treacherously With Me ... Saith The Lord.* ²¹ *A Voice Was Heard* upon the high places, *WEEPING* ... for they have perverted their way, and *They Have Forgotten The Lord Their God.* **Jeremiah 3: 3, 20-21 KJV**

Yes, Almighty God wept over the rebellion and the disloyalty of His Bride, Israel. Yet God, in His infinite mercy, forgave and remembered their sin no more.

> ... for I *will forgive* their iniquity, *and I will remember their sin no more.* **Jeremiah 31:34 KJV**

Even Jesus wept before His death when he looked out over Jerusalem; the home of God's Bride, Israel. And yet in His infinite mercy, He forgave Israel, and He forgave us; remembering our sins no more.

> *⁴¹As he approached Jerusalem and saw the city, he wept over it ⁴² and said, "If you, even you, had only known on this day what would bring you peace— but now it is hidden from your eyes.* **Luke 19:41-42**

The initial shock and awe and immediate anger of the reality of my current circumstances lasted about three years. Transplanting myself out of our suburban home and into the inner city to finish my college education, I actually moved back into the same building wherein I had met my husband. Remember, it was the diverse tenement with multifarious efficiencies and one room units that required the sharing of community kitchens and bathrooms just off the University of Minnesota's West Bank campus in Minneapolis. This location was perfect because I was attempting to finish my college degree. Here is where I resided until I graduated with a Bachelor of Science degree in Business Administration, major Accounting.

In the transplant of my revolt, the honesty, and innocence that God had been cultivating in my heart during my prior well protected life in Christian circles tended to attract all kinds of less than desirables. Men were tripping over themselves to give me attention. Whether it was good or bad attentiveness, my thirteen plus years of depravation was thriving on it. Unfortunately, my rebellion from God granted me no protection in my willful disobedient ***choices***. Unaccustomed to not having the activities of my three ring circus of a family surrounding me, and feeling stripped naked or rather, ***Abandoned in Divorce***, I found it very difficult to remain in my apartment alone. Hence, I sought companionship around as many people as possible. My tenement living environment assisted with that.

My anxiety related to these new surroundings, specifically associated with a limited budget, inner city noise and filth, as well as my many new academic demands propelled my stress level off of my personal Richter scale. I was allotted seven hundred dollars a month for rent and food for thirty six months until I completed school and snagged my first job. Some mutual investments from the divorce paid for my college tuition and books. My greatest form of gratitude was finding a penny on the sidewalk when walking to school. ***Abandoned in Divorce***, I recall finding hope in seeing a spindly dandelion determinedly emerging through the miles of concrete in my not so luscious surrounding. Admiring its efforts, I reflected that if the dandelion could make it in this concrete jungle, then I could as well. I was claiming the Scripture "I can do all things" but I was leaving God out of it at this time.

> *I can do all this through Him who gives me strength.* **Philippians 4:13**

The trauma of my transplant and now being ***Abandoned in Divorce***, made it near to impossible to eat. As soon as my stomach became aware that there was food in my mouth it began to cramp intensely. However, with not being able to eat, I had no problem drinking. One admirer supplied me with some form of protein drink when I started losing two pounds a day. For the sake of my Christian walk and with a family history of alcoholism, I had avoided alcohol in the past. However, with seven drinking establishments within crawling distance of my apartment, and many of the tenement dwellers faithful patrons of such and often straying in those directions, I decided to follow them into these many dens of iniquity and uncertainty.

Being **Abandoned in Divorce** and walking out from under the God's umbrella of protection in my rebellion certainly did not relieve the burdens of my **choices**. As a more mature student, and under the contexts of my present-day life style, it was difficult to participate in the full college experience. More often than not, the folks that I met in my local neighborhood or at school were not God fearing people. Surrounded by the homeless and the scholars, the drug addicts/dealers and the business owners, the alcoholics and the college students, the old and worn out and the mushrooming success stories, I was a lost little lamb who did not want to and/or could not go home. I was rebellious, lacked gratitude and now **Abandoned in Divorce**. Alas, there is a price to be paid for rebellion and lack of gratitude for all of God's many myriads of blessings.

> $_{62}$ *... because you did not obey the LORD your God.*
> ^{63} *Just as it pleased the LORD to make you prosper and increase in number, so it will please him to ruin and destroy you ...* **Deuteronomy 28:62-63**
>
> ^{47} *Because you did not serve the LORD your God joyfully and gladly in the time of prosperity, ^{48} therefore in hunger and thirst, in nakedness and dire poverty, you will serve the enemies the LORD*

> *sends against you. He will put an iron yoke on your neck ...* Deuteronomy 28:47-48

We take a lot for granted in this country, don't we? Even after I graduated in the ***abundance*** of a promising and flourishing career, I was still empty inside. Because of my disobedience, lack of gratitude and inconsistent personal walk with the Lord, I found myself miserable; ***But for God***! Struggling, but finally graduating, I fled the swirling spirits of destruction encamped against me. My inner city neighbors knew that I did not belong there. Many regulars from a particular drinking establishment purchased a going away cake for me which read, "Get out of here and get a job!". Many of them would never make it out, but I believe they saw God in me, in spite of how I was behaving.

> *"... The LORD does not look at the things people look at. People look at the outward appearance, but the LORD looks at the heart."* 1 Samuel 16:7

I would often ruminate on the fact that it might have been better had I stayed ***Abandoned in Marriage*** rather to have been exposed and endure the many challenges of being ***Abandoned in Divorce***? I had even asked my husband to take me back. That door was shut. Maybe he subconsciously was trying to get rid of me all along! I sound a bit like the Israelites who were whining to go back to Egypt after God had freed them from their slavery there!

> *No discipline seems pleasant at the time, but painful. Later on, however, it produces a harvest of righteousness and peace for those who have been trained by it.* Hebrews 12:11

As the years of my ***Abandoned in Divorce*** marched on with much pursuit by the opposite gender and great success in my career, I grappled to establish why I was still not enjoying my previous sweet fellowship with the Lord. Why was I not growing in my relationship with Him? Where was my passionate exultant joy and gratitude for all that God had done and was doing in my life? Why was He not restoring, as He had promised, "all the years that the locust had eaten"? As His Word says, there is never a joyful outcome when rebellion and lack of gratitude are present.

> *...I will restore to you the years that the locust hath eaten ... which I sent among you.* **Joel 2:25 KJV**

> *Be of good courage, and He shall strengthen your heart, all ye that hope in the Lord.* **Psalm 31:24 KJV**

As I pressed on in the absence of a joyful loving relationship with my husband, I would now focus on God's will for my life; seeking to find the joy of the Lord. Although not apparent to me at the time, the Potter was still with me; performing His perfect work. In His infinite mercy, God was breaking, melting and molding this jar of clay; fashioning me with His seal of approved workmanship.

> *For His anger lasts only a moment, but his favor lasts a lifetime; weeping may stay for the night, but rejoicing comes in the morning.* **Psalm 30:5**

Many years have passed on this journey to forgiveness and joy. It has only been in recent years that I can now articulate my current understanding of the Biblical meaning of and my actual receiving of the Fruit of the Spirit seed of joy as affectionately planted by Jesus in my heart's garden. **Freedom** from **condemnation** is just one of the many steps in my personal forgiveness journey. The resulting release of the joy produced is just one of the many blessings provided to each of us by Jesus, our Bride Groom, in our respective Fruit of the Spirit heart's garden. I was not **Abandoned in Divorce** by Him.

> *The voice of joy, and* the voice of *gladness, the voice of the bridegroom, and the voice of the bride,* the voice of them that *shall say, praise the Lord of hosts: for the Lord is good; for His mercy endureth for ever*: and of them that shall *bring the sacrifice of praise into the house of the Lord* ... Jeremiah 33:11 KJV

And so in my brokenness of the Master's melting and molding was birthed my Gratitude Book. Every evening, I recall and journal the many events of the day. I have a ***choice***. Am I going to focus on the negative, or am I going to rejoice in the positive as I again begin to trust in my new Husband, Jesus? He would never **Abandoned in Divorce**. Although all may have been instrumental, it would not be my ex-husband, or things, or people that would teach me about forgiveness and the many Fruits of the Spirit. It would be God! He would instruct me in how to trust Him and maintain His sustaining ***abundant*** love as I live now, **Abandoned in Divorce**.

> *You make known to me the path of life; you will fill me with joy in your presence, with eternal pleasures at your right hand.* Psalm 16:11

Purposing to concentrate on my many blessings, I ignore Satan's ***condemnations*** and guilt through diverse false accusations expressed through my family or children or church, or anything or anyone else. God had forgiven me. I was learning to receive and give forgiveness. I had asked all for forgiveness. The acts of forgiving me and receiving forgiveness from Him were now between others and Almighty God. My slate was washed clean in the blood of Jesus! No more ***condemnation***!

> *I tell you that in the same way there will be more rejoicing in heaven over one sinner who repents*

> *than over ninety-nine righteous persons who do not need to repent.* **Luke 15:7**

> *Therefore, there is now NO CONDEMNATION for those who are in Christ Jesus.* **Romans 8:1** (Emphasis supplied)

When we strip away our glitzy blinders and truly face the reality of the ***abundance*** of God's many blessings we take for granted in comparison to the bare bone necessities for survival, we begin to not only witness, but hail, with exultant joy, the bountiful provisions of our God.

> *The Lord is my strength and my shield; my heart trusted in Him, and I am helped: therefore my heart greatly rejoiceth; and with my song will I praise Him.* **Psalm 28:7 KJV**

Do we desire to be ***Abandoned into Abundance*** or remain ***Abandoned in Divorce***? Remember when I asked for joy nearing the end of my marriage? Well, one may truly arise from the ashes!

> **To appoint unto them that mourn in Zion, to give unto them beauty for ashes, the oil of joy for mourning, the garment of praise for the spirit of heaviness ... Isaiah 61:3 KJV**

In sincere acceptance and love, in adoring gratitude and praise, we may each release His joy. God did promise to never leave or forsake us; NEVER ***Abandoned by God***.

> *because God has said, "Never will I leave you; never will I forsake you."*[a] **Hebrews 13:5b**

> *... And surely I am with you always, to the very end of the age.* **Matthew 28:20b**

5 ABANDONED BY OUR CHURCH

> *... The LORD gives victory to his anointed. He answers him from his heavenly sanctuary with the victorious power of his right hand.* Psalm 20:6

Have we ever been de-fellowshipped or dis-fellowshipped, or in other words, *KICKED OUT* of our local church; **Abandoned by our Church**? Does this appear shocking to us? Maybe the events were not as extreme as that in our particular church relationships. However, possibly after our unwedded predicament or our divorce or our abortion or any other number of exposed shortcomings, there were a certain "few", or maybe, a certain "many" individuals in our church family who began to minimally interact with or, de-fellowship us. Perhaps they ceased to acknowledge us altogether. Did we feel **Abandoned by our Church**?

Was this body of believers who represent the Bride of Christ, our family's generational church? Maybe this was the church wherein we had accepted Jesus as our Lord and Savior? Were we married there? Was it the place of worship that stood in support when we baptized or dedicated our children to the Lord? Did we embark on various couple's marriage retreats there, sharing some of our deepest innermost secrets? Has this house of worship resolved to de-fellowship us or dis-fellowship us, or kick us out during a transition that is beyond our understanding? Where is the compassion of Jesus in all of that? Did He **Abandon His Church**?

> *The heart is deceitful above all things, and desperately wicked: who can know it?* Jeremiah 17:9 KJV

My husband and I began attending a marriage support group that our pastor had initiated perhaps eight months prior to the bottom falling out of our pretentious wedded bliss. We had been affiliated with this body of believers for about two years and had just withdrawn from the leadership of a 100 plus youth ministry. Hoping for a better outcome as related to the trials transpiring throughout our marriage, we also spent numerous occasions counseled by and prayed for with that church's pastor. However in my mind, all was lost when my hopes were finally dashed. The reality of my observation, and the emotional abuse faced through my husband's attempts to control me had sprouted a humongous weed bed of anger, bitterness, rebellion and divorce within my heart.

Initially aiming to be amicable for the children's sake, I had remained at the family home. Awaiting the divorce finalization, I purposed to maintain a somewhat balanced transition. My husband and children continued attending our family's place of worship. In the heat of my anger and rebellion, I no longer congregated there. One day, six couples from our marriage support group to include pastor and his wife, arrived on the front doorstep of our family home. They had come in love in an attempt to intervene. Without wanting to disclose the intimacy of the events that in their accumulation had caused me to surrender to the many impish minions sent from the gates of hell to destroy our marriage, I stood firm in my rebellious front so that all may see. Pastor was unimpressed with my display of revolt.

The reality is, I was not able to truly identify what had actually snapped and why; the root cause. I just remember what I saw, and I no longer wanted to hear another sermon, lecture, Scripture or encouraging word from any of them. I was mad at God and the lot of them.

> [18] *"Hear, you deaf; look, you blind, and see! ... [20] You have seen many things, but you pay no attention; your ears are open, but you do not listen."* Isaiah 42:18, 20

Prior to and through my re-location to the inner city, there were still a few individuals from church of whom I purposed to maintain contact. Others just tended to shy away altogether from any interaction with me. I attributed that to the fact that they were somewhat uncomfortable endeavoring with those who were experiencing some of life's greatest challenges; challenges that were out of their personal range of involvement. In retrospect, I have concluded that we each were probably formulating judgments regarding each of our behaviors, based on each of our actions as express through our personal interpretation of Biblical truth.

Who knows the work that our Maker God is undertaking in someone else's life when we witness others crisscrossing through complex occasions? Maybe upbringings or ignorance cause us to establish verdicts on facts wherein we may have very little understanding. Didn't Jesus come to save and to love; not to judge? Is that not the same Message for today? Has He **Abandoned His Church** that continues to sin to this day?

> *"A new command I give you: Love one another. As I have loved you, so you must love one another.* **John 13:34**

Just prior to the divorce settlement, I began seizing whatever form of attention I might attain in my mutiny. I began dating an artist/furnisher designer, and at that time, furniture factory owner. He resided in the same building wherein I had recently re-located. In a bit of irony, this was the same tenement that I had met my husband when I re-located from Canada. It was conveniently located across the street from the campus wherein I was to finish my degree. Able to nab one of the highly coveted inexpensive apartments in this building, this atheist artist along with some of his employees transported my belongings into my new inner city existence from my suburban family home.

One evening after returning from class and picking up a few groceries, my artist friend called me from his upstairs apartment. He promised to be down shortly, conveying that he had a surprise. After performing a quick organizational sweep of my apartment and upon responding to a knock at the door, I was taken aback to find pastor, his wife and several other couples from our marriage support group standing in the outer hallway of my apartment entrance.

As I welcomed the impromptu visitors into my studio flat, my atheist artist friend escaped hastily, smirking as he waved good bye over his shoulder. Apparently, he had been entertaining them in his not so clean bachelor dwelling, awaiting my arrival home. Another tenement friend had granted them access into the building, and realizing that I was not at my unit, he had directed them upstairs to my gentleman friend's residence. Pastor began by introducing each visitor should I have forgotten their names, and then opened in prayer. Next, he inquired further of my current living conditions. He spelled out that living with someone who was not our spouse in the Biblical sense of the term, was willful disobedience and rebellion. As my pastor, he had an obligation to present the facts of such rebellion to me as identified in the Scriptures. He commenced reading:

> *[15] "If your brother or sister[a] sins,[b] go and point out their fault, just between the two of you. If they listen to you, you have won them over. [16] But if they will not listen, take one or two others along, so that 'every matter may be established by the testimony of two or three witnesses.'[c]* **Matthew 18:15-16**

In case I happened to still not understand, the pastor expounded further offering that the Bible specifically furnishes instructions on how to deal with Christians who willfully keep on doing something seriously wrong; basically, for those who *choose* to continue in sin. As he had just read in Matthew 18:15-16, the Word of God confirms that for those who *choose* to follow in such rebellion, continually refusing to correct their willful disobedience despite all the efforts of others, the body of believers must follow certain steps. Specifically, and subsequent to fulfilling the above prescribed process, an announcement was to be made to the church body. As a result of that proclamation, should an individual still *choose* not to mend their ways, then that particular church body was to have no further interaction with that individual; as though that individual was no longer part of that church's family; ***Abandoned by our Church.***

> *If they still refuse to listen, tell it to the church; and if they refuse to listen even to the church, treat them as you would a pagan or a tax collector.*
> **Matthew 18: 17**

As the pastor more than highlighted, and as presented by Jesus from those verses during this confrontation, the intent of this process was to admonish or reprove one with cautioning or advising for their faults. I was not living with my husband, and the divorce was not final. However, I was not living with the artist either; maybe I was in the Biblical sense of the word. Should the church's discipline or admonition fail, and not produce corrective action on a sinner's part, then the church was to turn their back on that person. In this case, that would be me; ***Abandoned by my Church.***

The intent was to turn me, the sinner, over to the devil. By allowing Satan to have his way, permitted the Lord to have HIS way in the purification process of returning me to the church. The pastor was not trying to maintain the doctrine of a denomination, but rather, he was purposing to be a zealot in enforcing God's Word. As pastor of a suburban community church, he was attempting to discipline through the Word of God and I, was **Abandoned by my Church**. Rattling the little rebel within, pastor further outlined that the goal of the process was to protect the purity of the lives of those within the church from evil; a little leaven will invade the whole lot of bread if we are trying to keep it unleavened.

> *⁵ hand this man over to Satan for the destruction of the flesh,⁽ᵃ⁾⁽ᵇ⁾ so that his spirit may be saved on the day of the Lord. ⁶... Don't you know that a little yeast leavens the whole batch of dough? ⁷ Get rid of the old yeast, so that you may be a new unleavened batch—as you really are. For Christ, our Passover lamb, has been sacrificed. ⁸ Therefore let us keep the Festival, not with the old bread leavened with malice and wickedness, but with the unleavened bread of sincerity and truth. ⁹ I wrote to you in my letter not to associate with sexually immoral people—* **1 Corinthians 5:5-9**

It was vastly apparent at the time that this pastor took his job extremely seriously. Today, I understand his purpose. However, his approach applied combined with my defiant mindset ultimately resulted in a divorce from my church body as well; **Abandoned by our Church**. Should we **choose** to not learn our lessons, but rather continue in willful disobedience, then anticipate being **defellowshipped**. I was not at the church that Sunday for the final proclamation to my church family, but I believe God purposed to comfort me at the time with the following Scripture:

> *³ The teachers of the law and the Pharisees brought in a woman caught in adultery. They*

> *made her stand before the group ⁴and said to Jesus, "Teacher, this woman was caught in the act of adultery. ⁵In the Law Moses commanded us to stone such women. Now what do you say?" ... ⁷When they kept on questioning him, he straightened up and said to them, "Let any one of you who is without sin be the first to throw a stone at her." ... ⁹At this, those who heard began to go away one at a time, the older ones first, until only Jesus was left, with the woman still standing there.* John 8:3-5, 7, 9

The church was not deliberately trying to hurt me. The Word of God is indisputable. However, I do believe that the technique reflected by their actions may have begged a little refining. In order to fulfill His purpose for our lives, God's desire is that we remain obedient and cooperate with him in His refining process. That does not mean that we must be sinless before we can hear from God. None of us our sinless as demonstrated in the above Scripture; for **ALL** have sinned! That is why Jesus shed His blood on the cross; that none are lost. He became our sin and washed us white as snow by His blood. However, in my rebellious state, I was not ***choosing*** to listen. God yearns to commune with us through His Word. Maybe that is why He reminded me of this particular portion of Scripture at that time. Remember, He loves us with an everlasting love.

> ¹⁰ *Jesus straightened up and asked her, "Woman, where are they? Has no one condemned you?" ¹¹"No one, sir," she said. "Then neither do I condemn you," Jesus declared. "Go now and leave your life of sin."* John 8:10-11

Prior to this final landslide, my husband and I had also started counseling with a highly regarded Christian therapist who was also credentialed as an expert witness. My husband discontinued seeing him after I moved out of the house. However for sanity's sake, I continued to seek his wisdom through my initial transition. I will never forget the day wherein he told me that I was going to lose no matter which ***choice*** I selected; staying with a husband who had **Abandoned in Marriage** or, stepping forth into my new life and becoming **Abandoned in Divorce**. The reality of his spoken words became a truth in my present day reality. However, that truth would become tools of refinement in Jesus, our eternal Husband's hands. He is faithful and never gives up on us. He never gave up on me.

He remained my glimmering Light through the many dark passages that I was to travel. Jesus IS the Light of my life! He is available to be the Light of each of our lives. We can purpose, with God's grace, to become pure in thought, word, and deed; allowing Him to clean up our acts through His Word! Jesus teaches our hearts His will though mediation on His Word. We have a ***choice*** as to whether we will ***choose*** to have pure thoughts, pure feelings and pure self-controlled emotions under the power of the Holy Spirit. We can clean the filth out of our clothes but it is more challenging when it comes to our habitual or recurring sins. It is our thoughts, words, decisions and desires that often interfere with a truly pure heart. We longs for us to think what He thinks, desire what He desires, hate what He hates, and love what He loves.

> ... Look not on his countenance, or on the height of his stature; ... *for the Lord seeth not as man seeth; for man looketh on the outward appearance, but the Lord looketh on the heart.* 1 Samuel 16:7 KJV

Are we not grateful that God looks at our hearts and not at our external achievements, appearances, behaviors, or failures? Jesus does not reward education, intellect, business success, or social position, as the world does. It is God Who must clean the rest of us up for His purpose.

Pride will only get in the way if we think we can do it ourselves. My life is a prime example of that promise. God alone is able to raise up beauty out of the ashes.

> *To appoint unto them that mourn in Zion, to give unto them beauty for ashes, the oil of joy for mourning, the garment of praise for the spirit of heaviness; that they might be called trees of righteousness, the planting of the Lord, that he might be glorified.* **Isaiah 61:3 KJV**

In spite of our short comings, let us praise and thank God for His plan to create and save us, His children from ourselves and our blatant sins! He has known each of us from the beginning of time. He knows who will ***choose*** Him and be like Him. God has loved each of us with an everlasting love. His ever patient agape love is ever available to redeem us with the blood of Jesus. Jesus is ever ready to purify us through His Word.

> **For whom he did foreknow, he also did predestinate to be conformed to the image of his Son, that he might be the firstborn among many brethren. Romans 8:29**

God longs to change us into the image and likeness of His Son; to make us like Jesus. When we accept Him as our Lord and Savior, we are launched onto a mission; a mission to learn how to completely surrender ourselves to Jesus. Through our obedience, and as we put our entire faith and trust in Him, God is able to supernaturally regenerate us; making us new. Now we are a brand new creation as God's Word says:

> *... if any man be in Christ, he is a NEW creature: old things are passed away; behold, ALL THINGS ARE BECOME NEW.* **2 Corinthians 5:17 KJV**

> [26] *A new heart also will I give you, and a new spirit will I put within you: and I will take away the*

> *stony heart out of your flesh, and I will give you an heart of flesh.* ²⁷ *And I will put my spirit within you* ... **Ezekiel 36:26-27 KJV**

Yes, we may have been **Abandoned by our Church**. That church family may have de-fellowshipped us, or dis-fellowshipped us, or kicked us out, **but for God**! He has a purpose. Where was Jesus in all of that? Waiting for this time; waiting for us to turn the corner; waiting for us to receive ***His will be done on earth as it is in heaven***; waiting for us to perform His purpose in each of our hearts. Why? Jesus wants to walk arm-in-arm with us on the road to spiritual purity, growth, maturity, and strength. He longs for our surrender so that He might guide, teach and show us what our purpose and mission is, and how to do it. ***His will be done on earth as it is in heaven***!

> **Blessed are the pure in heart: for they shall see God. Matthew 5:8 KJV**

And what is the reward? We shall see God! We shall see God in the outside world, in His creation, in His children, and in the faces of those we are to introduce to Him whom have yet not met Him, those whom He has known from the beginning of time. Oh, it hurts being *Kicked Out* of the church; when they ripped off the bandage to expose the festering impure infection that may have been breeding within our life. However, the pain of that exposure has allowed the Light of Jesus' Word to purify and heal that infection. For by that, we may, like prodigal sons or daughters, returned home to the arms of our *God Father*.

Have we still not learned who we are through our relationship with God? Shall we allow Him to define who we are and not others? Meeting ourselves for the first time, are we not meeting God face to face and allowing Him to tell us who we are? And seeing His face, shall we not permit Him to work His purpose in our lives?

> *And we all, who with unveiled faces contemplate[a] the Lord's glory, are being transformed into his image with ever-increasing glory, which comes from the Lord, who is the Spirit.* **2 Corinthians 3:18**

Where are we on this journey to fulfill ***His will be done on earth as it is in heaven***? What will be our potential outcome? Will we have to turn back and do a few more laps, only to eventually cry out once again in repentance and seeking mercy? Through our personal failures, have we still not recognized that God has never failed us, but rather, enveloped us in His arms? Is He not ever setting our paths straight and subsequently giving us the desires of our hearts?

Do we now recognize the ***abundance*** of His grace bestowed upon us and the ***abundance*** of His grace that we each are to give back for ***His will to be done on earth as it is in heaven***? Do we desire to be ***Abandoned into Abundance*** or to remain ***Abandoned by our Church***? Have we not yet recognize that our new command is to love as we have experienced His love? After all, God did promise to never leave or forsake us. He will NEVER ***Abandon His Church***.

> *... because God has said, "Never will I leave you; never will I forsake you."[a]* **Hebrews 13:5b**

> *... And surely I am with you always, to the very end of the age.* **Matthew 28:20b**

6   ABANDONING OUR CHILDREN

It is God who arms me with strength[a] and keeps my way secure. **2 Samuel 22:33**

What were the circumstances that resulted in us physically, mentally, emotionally or spiritually ***Abandoning our Children***? Were we unable to relate because we too had been ***Abandoned at Conception*** or ***Abandoned in Adolescence***? Did we find no role model that might take us aside to teach us how to be a good or Godly mother or father? Maybe the crippling guilt of rejection and failure stemming from being ***Abandoned in Marriage***, ***Abandoned in Divorce*** or ***Abandoned by our Church*** has released penetrating perplexing anguish from both within and without?

We may have encountered ourselves to be not only insensitive to the feelings of others near and dear to us, but desensitized within ourselves by the ever changing tides of what we were enduring. Potentially in the short-term or possibly long-term, we may have discovered ourselves floating adrift in a sea of ***condemnation*** and lack of self-worth? Conceivably feeling ***Abandoned by God*** in our spiritually immature or not so immature state, we may have lashed out at Him in anger.

Did we lose ourselves in the whirlwinds of our realities that were encompassing us at the time? Bound and incapacitated by melancholy, did we emotionally detach ourselves for our own preservation? Had we ***chosen*** rather to seek release from the distress and regret in a bottle of alcohol, pills, a pipe, or a "Twinkie"? Were we clenching our last shred of demonstrative well-being, leaving nothing by which to comfort and nurture our own children?

There have been many women throughout the course of time who have relinquished their children for any number of painfully complex and arduously obscure conflicts. There are others however who may have had no explanations for their forfeiture reasoning. In all cases, the reality of **Abandoning our Children** would impact the deepest fiber of each emotion of all parties affected. Although the terms of surrender may contrast our life's journey, the Word of God provides a number of examples of mothers who have yielded their children; **Abandoning our Children**.

The first example that comes to mind is that of the biological mother of Moses. There within the pages of the first and second Book of Exodus, we uncover a new king reigning over Egypt. He has no interest in how the Israelite Joseph had saved his county in its historic famine. Remember, Joseph was sold by his brothers; **Abandoned in Adolescence**. However God, in His great purpose and plans for Joseph, caused all things to work together for good through Joseph during that drought.

This new king was apprehensively realizing that the Israelites have become far too numerous in his country. Contemplating the fact that should a war break out, the Israelites might join Egypt's enemies, and fight against them, the king assigned slave masters over the Israelites to enforce some form of subservient control. He would oppress them with forced labor. Should they leave his country, who would perform all the toil?

Soon, the Egyptians came to dread the Israelites even more. No matter how they endeavored to oppress them, the Israelites continued to multiply. Ruthlessly working them in brick and mortar and in all other forms of field labor, the king strove to make their lives crueler with more punitive labor. In addition, the Egyptian king ordered the Hebrew midwives to kill all the Hebrew baby boys at birth.

The midwives who feared God did not do what the king had commanded. They simply made excuses that the Hebrew women were vigorous and would often give birth before their arrival. As such, the Hebrews continued to increase. Finally, irritated Pharaoh gave an edict to all of his people that required them to kill every newly birthed Hebrew child. The male babies were to be thrown into the Nile and submerged to their death. However, every female child birthed was permitted to live.

Baby Moses' father was a Levite, one of Joseph's brothers from the twelve tribes of Israel. After their marriage, Moses' mother who was also from the house of Levi conceived several children. Her third child, Moses, was born after the king's decree. She was initially able to hide him, but after several months, she indirectly complied with the king's decree. Instead of throwing the baby into the Nile to his death as ordered, she placed the child into the Nile in an ark basket made of bulrushes and sealed with pitch. Was he a product of **Abandoning our Children**?

> *and we know that in all things God works for the good of those who love him, who[a] have been called according to his purpose.* **Romans 8:28**

She placed the basket in the long grasses next to the river's edge. Dispatching the baby's older sister Miriam to see what would become of him, the girl followed the floating nest at a nearby distance. And in God's infinite plan, the daughter of Pharaoh ***just happened*** to be down at the river bathing. One of her maidens ***just happened*** to walk along by the river's edge to see the ark floating among the long grasses. Sending her maid to fetch it, Pharaoh's daughter opened the ark, and exposed the child.

As baby Moses began to cry, Pharaoh's daughter's heart melted with compassion at the sight of him. On hearing the princess dispatch her maid to secure a nurse to feed the child, Miriam who *just happened* to still be watching over all of these happenings, popped out of her concealed site and directed the maid to her mother, Moses' mother.

Was God not in control? Moses' mother was not only able to continue to care for her son legally under the control of Pharaoh's daughter, but she also earned a wage for looking after him! As Moses grew, his mother yielded him completely to Pharaoh's daughter wherein he became the princess' son. Was Moses the product of **Abandoning our Children**?

Yes, but what were the circumstances that caused this mother to give up her cherished gift? Had God not preordained or *chosen* Moses in advance to lead the Israelites out of the bondage of Egypt and into the Promised Land? God had a purpose for placing Moses into this new family. What would our opinion have been on that situation had we not had all the facts; the mind of God?

> *For my thoughts are not your thoughts, neither are your ways my ways, saith the Lord.* **Isaiah 55:8 KJV**

Samuel was another child that was given up by his mother. Was he also a product of **Abandoning our Children**? In I Samuel 1, we discover Hannah taunted and tormented by her husband's other wife, Peninnah. She has many children, but poor barren despairing Hannah was often seen pleading with God for a child, for she had none. Her husband Elkanna annually took the family for worship and sacrifice to the temple at Shiloh. Even though the Lord had not blessed them with a child, he loved Hannah very much.

One day after arriving at the temple, Hannah fasted and wept and pleaded before God for a child. During this homily, Hannah pledged a vow to the Lord. Should He grant her a man child, she would set him apart, banning any razor near his head as was the custom of one set apart. Ultimately, she promised to offer the child back to the Lord. Now the elderly temple priest at the time named Eli, witnessed Hannah seeming to be speaking to God in her heart. Her lips were moving, but no sound was coming out of her vocal cords.

Eli initially thought she was drunk; another inaccurate judgment by one who does not have all the facts! Been there and done that at both ends of the judgment; giving and receiving! Addressing Hannah with this false assumption, Hannah quickly corrected Eli, submitting to him that she is a woman with a sorrowful spirit; not drunk! In reality, she was pouring out her soul before the Lord for a son. On hearing this, Eli advised Hannah to depart in peace, prophesizing that God would grant her petition.

> *² "I know that you can do all things; no purpose of yours can be thwarted. ³ ... Surely I spoke of things I did not understand, things too wonderful for me to know.* **Job 42:2-3**

Hannah returned home, became pregnant, and at his birth, named her son, Samuel. When he was weaned, she took Samuel to Eli, the priest. Reminding Eli of her prior petition to the Lord, she yielded the child to God as vowed. Hannah left little Samuel in the custody of Eli, an old man with two rowdy carousing adult sons. Was God in control? Was Samuel a product of ***Abandoning our Children***?

Was Samuel not the one who anointed both Saul and David to be kings in Israel? Not having the mind of God and not having all the facts, what would our judgment have been in that situation? God had a divine purpose for Samuel. In the heart wrenching pain of relinquishing and separating herself from her most cherish gift on earth, Hannah submitted to the will of God. Did she ever recognize the ultimate anointed and appointed purpose for her son's life because of her obedience? Was he a product of ***Abandoning our Children***? And in all of this, what did Hannah do? She praised her God.

> *¹ ... "My heart rejoices in the LORD; in the LORD my horn[a] is lifted high. My mouth boasts over my enemies, for I delight in your deliverance. ² "There is no one holy like the LORD; there is no one besides you; there is no Rock like our God. ³ "Do not keep talking so proudly or let your mouth speak such arrogance, for the LORD is a God who knows, and by him deeds are weighed ... ⁹ He will guard the feet of his faithful servants, but the wicked will be silenced in the place of darkness ...* 1 Samuel 2: 1-3, 9

Hannah praised God in the midst of this cleaving chasm of separation. Did she feel jubilant and joyful? Probably not, but she trusted her God and praised Him anyway. In reality, our children are not our own; they are a gift from God. Many of us have dedicated or baptized our children to God. Our children are given to us to rear in the nurture and admonition of Him. He has entrusted them to our care to teach them about Him so that they too may receive forgiveness for their sins and commit their lives to performing ***His will be done on earth as it is in heaven***.

> *... instead, bring them up in the training and instruction of the Lord.* **Ephesians 6:4**

Sometimes we are required to make tough decisions or, through God's foreordained intervention, they are made for us. Either way, the reality of the resulting agony and anguish for any parent or child, with the prevailing forces and outcomes on each mentally, physically, emotionally and spiritually, are more often than not, insurmountable; ***But***

for God. He knows that each of us are but flesh. He made us with emotions and we are often weak. He is aware that we will crack and break; especially when He is not made Lord of our lives.

> *But he said to me, "My grace is sufficient for you, for my power is made perfect in weakness." Therefore I will boast all the more gladly about my weaknesses, so that Christ's power may rest on me.*
> **2 Corinthians 12:9**

However, He has a plan to break and melt and mold us anyway! Even when He is Lord of our lives, things happen; ***But for God***. He is in control! He has a plan for each of us, and the separation and removal of a child from our lives may be part of God's divine plan. We saw this in Joseph's life. He was removed from His parents, his country and everything that was familiar to him and became a slave. ***But for God***, Joseph became a savior during the famine. Such was the case with Moses. He was the savior that led the Israelites out of bondage to the door of God's Promised Land. We do not have all the facts. We do not have the mind of God. And ***ALL*** things work together for good. He started this work in our lives in His preplanning, and He has already seen the finish.

> *The LORD will vindicate me; your love, LORD, endures forever— do not abandon the works of your hands.* **Psalm 138:8**

> *and we know that in all things God works for the good of those who love him, who[a] have been called according to his purpose.* **Romans 8:28**

> *The LORD's right hand is lifted high; the LORD's right hand has done mighty things!"* **Psalm 118:16**

Striving to maintain some semblance of normalcy for the children after the divorce, my plan was for my husband to move out, with only me and the children remaining in our suburban home. In an attempt to expedite my entry into employment upon graduation, the strategy was to juggle the children's schedules whilst driving into the inner city to attend college full time. With that agenda, there would be little to no time for supplemental employment wherein to fund extra support to enable staying in the family home.

However, through divorce negotiations, this was not acceptable to my husband for this resolve would require a significant increase in support from him. With no workable determination, and in my rebellion to finally be released from his control and manipulation, I propelled the most difficult decision of my life. Nothing would have prepared me for the devastation that this cascading waterfall of destruction would effect on so many lives.

I had been a stay-at-home mother and had immersed myself in providing the perfect Christian life for my family. As with most parents, I wanted them to have a better upbringing and opportunities than I had so severely judged my parents for not providing me. From the point of our first child's conception, my primary purpose was perfecting and protecting their lives and the process. Obsessed with both their internal as well as their external growth and development, to include shelter from any negative forces and influences, I encapsulated the children to the best of my ability in the parameters of that existence. To my husband's dismay, out the door went the TV.

Preparing for natural childbirths and breastfeeding, I also strove to safeguard their little bottoms by hand rinsing their cloth diapers four rinses following wringer washing. Heating with our own fire wood, growing our own food, and making our own clothes, with church family as our central interaction, I purposed to shelter the children in our guarded rural environment. When the critical decision for education arrived, we ***chose*** to home school. Safe from harm, I wanted control over the development of these perfect specimens in my Petri dish.

Apparent to all, my principal focus was the well-being of my children. In spite of being **Abandoned in Marriage**, they had empowered me to remain steady for as long as I had. At the time I was **Abandoned in Divorce**, our daughter was ten and a half years and our son was almost eight years of age. The divorce was having a major impact on their lives under normal circumstance. However, in my attempt to maintain their stability in their same beds, in their same house, in their same neighborhood, in their same church, and with a greater provision of funding and constancy of their father, I made the ***choice*** to remove myself and leave the children with my husband in the family home. Was I **Abandoning my Children**?

In my selfishness, should I have dragged them into an impoverished concrete jungle existence, with nothing but traffic and parking lots far and wide to play in and around? Would the ever changing environment of transients, and multicultural students been a better place for these precious plants to thrive in their development? I was not even sure of what I was doing mentally, physically, emotionally and spiritually at this point in time. Must they endure my drastic transition? Was I **Abandoning my Children**? What was God's plan for their lives?

> *Man's goings are of the Lord; how can a man then understand his own way?* **Proverbs 20:24 KJV**

And so the pronouncement was made wherein the children were informed that they were to remain in the family home with their father. They would visit me, their mother, only every other weekend. They had rarely been left with a babysitter. Stripped naked of all that I held most dear to me, I embarked on attaining a college education in a hodge-podge of an ever changing people, life-styles, attitudes, religions and education; a melting pot of settings of which I had no idea as to how I was to acclimatize.

As I have expanded on in **Chapter 5, ABANDONED IN DIVORCE**, I was unaccustomed to not having the activities of my three ring circus surrounding me. Abandoned and alone whether by **choice** or not, I would often find it very difficult to remain in my apartment. Seeking companionship by being surrounded by as many people as possible, my new tenement existence was a definite plus in relieving that loneliness. However, the anxiety related to these new surroundings, a limited budget, inner city noise and filth, as well as my many new academic demands, propelled my stress level right off of my personal Richter scale.

Being **Abandoned in Divorce** combined with the stress trauma of my transplant had plainly made it impossible for me to eat. I had avoided alcohol in the past; however, with seven drinking establishments in the area, and with many of my neighborhood faithful patrons of such, I **chose** to follow them into these many dens of iniquity. Being **Abandoned in Divorce** and walking out from under God's umbrella of protection and into this ring of rebellion did not help matters much either. Under the present circumstances, and being a more mature student, it was difficult to go through the full college experience. More often than not, the folks that I met in my immediate neighborhood or at school were not God fearing people. Surrounded by so many variables, I was a lost little lamb who did not want to and/or could not go home.

The children's innocence and welcoming spirits launched forth initially with a willingness to adapt to the shattering perfectionism that had attempted to mold their little lives.

They had been raised to this point in the purity and perfection of the love of Christ in the shielded circles that surrounded them. I was a child of God, but His Light was not shining to my children or anyone else in this torrent of sin that I had moved into, and was witnessing and acting upon. We were encircled with chaos.

> *[1] As for you, you were dead in your transgressions and sins, [2] in which you used to live when you followed the ways of this world and of the ruler of the kingdom of the air, the spirit who is now at work in those who are disobedient. [3] All of us also lived among them at one time, gratifying the cravings of our flesh[a] and following its desires and thoughts ...* **Ephesians 2:1-3**

One day on a weekend wherein my children were visiting, my son and I were walking across one of the many parking lots in my concrete habitation. After the divorce was finalized, I returned to my maiden name. My eight year old son had become aware of that event during the previous week. As we navigated through the maze of cars, he in essence declared that I was no longer part of their family any more. I no longer had the same last name. Yes, I was hurt and stunned. However, in my next breath I assuredly responded to him, emphasizing that he grew in my body and came out of that same body. He was made within me and his body contains half of who I am. We are and will always be family! ***But for God***. As I have noted before, there is always a price that one must pay for rebellion and lack of gratitude for all of God's many myriads of blessings.

Both the children and I would pay that price. We each witness things that I never imagined would ever be part of their respective life's cycle. I did things that I never dreamed would mold their individual processes of becoming. Their lives had gone from perfectionism to carelessness. How was a child to absorb that? ***But for God***.

> *⁴ But because of his great love for us, God, who is rich in mercy, ⁵ made us alive with Christ even when we were dead in transgressions—it is by grace you have been saved. ... ⁸ For it is by grace you have been saved, through faith—and this is not from yourselves, it is the gift of God— ⁹ not by works, so that no one can boast.* Ephesians 2:4-5, 8-9

To this day there remain many scars from the events that were to become the molds that would impact the shape of my children's lives; and my life for that matter. As with Hannah, these were my gifts from God. But I had not been a good steward with these gifts that He had entrusted into my hands. I had relinquished control, and had been convicted, like many others, of **Abandoning our Children**. God commands us to teach our children about His greatness when they are young. That I endeavored to do, and as such, I am grateful.

> *Start children off on the way they should go, and even when they are old they will not turn from it.*
> Proverbs 22:6

His Word also says that if we have purposed *to train up our children*, then, *when they are old, they will not depart from it*! With both children now adults in their mid-thirties, they are presently reflecting Jesus and their lessons learned to the next generation by their respective life's examples. I had asked God and my children for forgiveness. I have forgiven myself. **But for God**! No longer burden by my sin which is forgiven and forgotten by God, and removed *as far as the east is from the west*, I rejoice in His mercy and grace!

> *As far as the east is from the west, so far has he removed our transgressions from us.* Psalm 103:12

> *Therefore, there is now NO CONDEMNATION for those who are in Christ Jesus.* Romans 8:1 (Emphasis supplied)

God is the author and the finisher of our lives through each of our repentances and restorations. He has a purpose for each of us. We are here to accomplish ***His will to be done on earth as it is in heaven***.

> *... there will be more rejoicing in heaven over one sinner who repents than over ninety-nine righteous persons who do not need to repent.* Luke 15:7

But for God, Who has washed away all of our sins, even those that in the closeness of our prior fellowship's we never imagined to be in our site. He patiently waits, and gently and sometimes not so gently nudges us to carry on in His grace. Omniscient, omnipotent, omnipresent God knew ***ALL***! And yet, He still works ***ALL*** things to His purpose for ***His will to be done on earth as it is in heaven***. Do we desire to be ***Abandoned into Abundance*** or to remain in the ***condemnation*** and grief associated with ***Abandoning our Children***? In adoring gratitude and praise for our Father's love, did He not promise never to leave us and to never forsake us; NEVER ***Abandoned by God***? ***His will to be done on earth as it is in heaven***.

> *... because God has said, "Never will I leave you; never will I forsake you."*[a] Hebrews 13:5b

> *... And surely I am with you always, to the very end of the age.* Matthew 28:20b

7 ABANDONED BY ABORTION

> [1] *Have mercy on me, O God, according to your unfailing love; according to your great compassion blot out my transgressions.* [2] *Wash away all my iniquity and cleanse me from my sin.* [3] *For I know my transgressions, and my sin is always before me.* [4] *Against you, you only, have I sinned and done what is evil in your sight ...*
> **Psalm 51:1-4**

Maybe through no fault of our own, or by our own actions, we discovered ourselves to be with child; pregnant and possibly panicking. Were we raped by a stranger, an uncle, our father or a cousin? Currently, we may be in high school, ready to graduate from college, progressing on the most amazing career path or, we may be already overburdened with too many mouths to feed. In spite of our spiritual convictions, and in that panic of, or in the instability of our insecurity and uncertainty or, possibly following some premeditated rationale, a resolution had been established wherein we made a ***choice*** to terminate the pregnancy; to ***Abandoned by Abortion***.

Wisely, we may never have to revisit making that decision again. Through God's infinite mercy and grace, we have received His forgiveness and forgiven ourselves. We now purpose to leave the circumstances of that conception behind, along with the facts surrounding the sins that may be encapsulated in that entire situation. Confessing our sins has washed them in the blood of Jesus. When God looks at us now, He sees us as white as snow. Our sins are now removed by Him ***"as far as the east is from the west"***. He remembers them no more. We too must purpose to remember them no more also.

> *... though your sins be as scarlet, they shall be as white as snow; though they are red like crimson, they shall be like wool.* **Isaiah 1:18**

> *as far as the east is from the west, so far has he removed our transgressions from us.* **Psalm 103:12**

However, for some of us, that free **choice** that seemed justified at the time, may presently be plaguing us; constricting us in the bondage of **condemnation** for this act wherein we have **Abandoned by Abortion**. We may not in actuality know the pre-ordained date that God had assigned as the child's birth date. Nevertheless, we more frequently than not, reflect in our approximations, as to what date that might have been. In addition, we may mull over the potential sex of the child; would we have birthed a ballerina or a ball player? As well, we might annually or when mused upon, envision the development of said child; possibly performing a quick calculation, we may consider what the child's current age and skillset would have been.

One evening, King David who already had a few wives, saw Bathsheba, wife of his neighbor and mighty warrior Uriah, bathing on her rooftop. Uriah was presently on the front line in David's military. Lusting after Uriah's wife's beauty, David sought to have her sexually. Sending his men to fetch her to his palace, David had intimate relations with her. When David was finished with her, she was returned to her home. We do not hear Bathsheba's side of the story in these statements of facts found in 2 Samuel 11. David was the king and when his men were sent to her home and she was told that the king requested her presence, she probably did not have a **choice** to refuse.

When Bathsheba became aware that she was pregnant with David's child, she notified the king. We know the child is David's for Bathsheba's husband is away at war. Upon receiving her announcement of the pregnancy, David strategized to cover his tracts by ordering her husband, Uriah home from the battle front. His deceptive plan, anticipated that Uriah would have relations with his wife on his return home. Then David's child would be identified as Uriah's, and not the fruit of his coming together with Uriah's wife. In other words, David was expecting to be able to conceal his relations with Bathsheba, and the resulting ***abundance*** conceived would be claimed as Uriah's child.

However, David's plan was soon to be foiled. Uriah, in his commitment to the cause of the fight, and understanding the hardships that his men were currently enduring on the battlefront, declined to take the liberty of enjoining himself with his wife whilst the troops were still battling in the fields. Hearing of this, David even commanded Uriah to remain at home one more night. David connived to have Uriah feast with him at the palace. David was purposing to get Uriah drunk at the banquet, hoping then that Uriah might sleep with his wife. Unfortunately for David, at the conclusion of the feast and in Uriah's drunkenness, he only managed to stumble down and slumber where the king's servants slept. He never returned to Bathsheba.

Over the centuries, every age has had its various methods to terminate unwanted pregnancy. Those thoughts are not evidenced by David here in the Scriptures. Although David's child was not ***Abandoned by Abortion***, David did have an alternative plan; someone's life was to be terminated. David's scheme was to send Uriah purposely to the front line to fight. This dispatch would ensure that Uriah would be killed. With Uriah's death forthcoming, David would be free to protect his *"**little secret**"* by merely adding Bathsheba to his list of wives.

After Uriah's death and Bathsheba's mourning period, David received Bathsheba into the palace as his new bride.

She bore David the son of their "***little secret***". David came to love Bathsheba intensely over that period of time. There was the usual celebration of joy and exuberance exhibited at the birth of the child. However, it would not be long after the child's delivery that there would be countless days and nights of deep despair with much prayer and fasting on David's part. Why, because God had passed judgment on David for his actions. Nathan, the prophet, came to David with a message from God:

> *¹¹ "This is what the LORD says: 'Out of your own household I am going to bring calamity on you. Before your very eyes I will take your wives and give them to one who is close to you, and he will sleep with your wives in broad daylight. ¹² You did it in secret, but I will do this thing in broad daylight before all Israel.'" ¹³ Then David said to Nathan, "I have sinned against the LORD." Nathan replied, "The LORD has taken away your sin. You are not going to die. ¹⁴ But because by doing this you have shown utter contempt for[a] the LORD, the son born to you will die."* **2 Samuel 12:11-14**

The dreadfully ill child of David and Bathsheba's union finally yielded and died. Although the child was not **Abandoned by Abortion** through human hands, David did lose the child because of the sins that surrounded this coming together. During the child's illness, David spent endless days and nights, lying prostrate on the ground before the Lord. He did not eat, nor bath, nor change his clothes, nor sleep. He would just lay interceding and pleading before God for the life of his child. And he prayed:

> *⁶ Yet you desired faithfulness even in the womb; you taught me wisdom in that secret place. ⁷ Cleanse me with hyssop, and I will be clean; wash me, and I will be whiter than snow. ⁸ Let me hear joy and gladness; let the bones you have crushed*

rejoice. ⁹ Hide your face from my sins and blot out all my iniquity. ¹⁰ Create in me a pure heart, O God, and renew a steadfast spirit within me. ¹¹ Do not cast me from your presence or take your Holy Spirit from me. ¹² Restore to me the joy of your salvation and grant me a willing spirit, to sustain me. ¹³ Then I will teach transgressors your ways, so that sinners will turn back to you. ¹⁴ Deliver me from the guilt of bloodshed, O God, you who are God my Savior, and my tongue will sing of your righteousness. **Psalm 51:6-14**

In the guilt that surrounds our **choice**, **Abandoned by Abortion**, are we too, pleading before the Lord. Are we ever requesting mercy for our action; laying incapacitated on the floor before God in our own **condemnation** because of the option that we selected? Shall we not arise from under this burden of **condemnation** and receive God's forgiveness and mercy? So despondent was David, as expressed through these many endless days of supplication that when the child finally breathed his last breath, returning to the bosom of the Lord from which it came, David's staff were afraid to reveal that occurrence to him. And David prayed:

¹⁵ Open my lips, Lord, and my mouth will declare your praise. ¹⁶ You do not delight in sacrifice, or I would bring it; you do not take pleasure in burnt offerings. ¹⁷ My sacrifice, O God, is[a] a broken spirit; a broken and contrite heart you, God, will not despise. **Psalm 51:15-17**

Are family and friends afraid to comfort us, to walk with us, and to offer relief for us wherein we may place our **condemnation** and guilt at the foot of the cross? Jesus paid it all; for yesterday, for today and for tomorrow; all sin! Although David had not **Abandoned by Abortion**, two termination of life had transpired because of these "***little secrets***" or concealed sins, Uriah and the male child.

> *For the wages of sin is death; but the gift of God is eternal life through Jesus Christ our Lord.* **Romans 6:23 KJV**

Are we afraid to approach people with our *"little secret"* that we have hidden in our cages of bondage? Is it possible that such revelation will only increase the already unrelenting tides of **condemnation** continually engulfing us? Do we refuse to accept the healing counsel of their ministering words because we anticipate through Satan's whispered lies in our ear, more judgment and not healing?

> *[13] Be pleased, O Lord, to deliver me: O Lord, make haste to help me. [14] Let them be ashamed and confounded together that seek after my soul to destroy it; let them be driven backward and put to shame that wish me evil. [15] Let them be desolate for a reward of their shame that say unto me, Aha, aha.* **Psalm 40:13-15 KJV**

Do others compassionately desire to seek our restoration through the application of the healing Balm of Gilead; speaking life into our journey by professing God's living encouraging and strengthening Word? If we have accepted Jesus free gift of Salvation then we have confessed our sins? Have we not received that forgiveness, with our sins washed clean, removed, forgotten, *as far as the east is from the west, to be remembered no more*?

> *If we confess our sins, he is faithful and just to forgive us our sins, and to cleanse us from all unrighteousness.* **1 John 1:9 KJV**

If we have asked Jesus to come into our heart, to forgive us for ***ALL*** of our sins, and to take over Lordship of our life, then, we are a child of the King! We have been washed in the blood of the Lamb. Yes, we will fall into a mud puddle of sin now and again, but we are righteous and clean because of what Jesus ***already did on the Cross***. He paid for ***ALL*** of our sins; even the sins we will commit tomorrow. God now sees each of us only as ***white as snow*** through the blood of His Son, Jesus.

What each of us, and again, speaking from my experience, and as observed through David's actions here in the Scriptures, what we are actually struggling with in all of this turmoil is our pride.

> *... "My grace is sufficient for you, for my power is made perfect in weakness." Therefore I will boast all the more gladly about my weaknesses, so that Christ's power may rest on me.* **2 Corinthians 12:9**

If the devil can hook his line into our pride, then all he has left to do is lure us in to his accusations feast of ***condemnation***. *What kind of Christian are you; you killed your own child; what if people find out your "little secret"*, etc., etc., etc. Do we not yet understand that when we confess our sins God removes them ***as far as the east in from the west, and He remembers them no more***? Then why do we keep remembering this event? We are no longer guilty. Remember, the price has been paid for ***ALL*** of our sins; even those sins we will execute tomorrow. If we fall short half an hour later then we will confess those sins. But the fact of the matter is that ***ALL*** of our sins were nailed to the cross that day at Calvary. With what right, as children of the most high God, does Satan have to torment us, to ***condemn*** us? Doesn't God's Word say?

> *having canceled the charge of our legal indebtedness, which stood against us and condemned us; he has taken it away, nailing it to the cross.* **Colossians 2:14**

> *Therefore, there is now no condemnation to them who are in Christ Jesus.* **Romans 8:1**

Our departed child, as with David's son, has returned to the bosom of our God. After days of deepest despair and sleepless prayer and fasting, David lost the child of that coming together. For whatever reason, we too may have lost a child of a coming together. However, this was not the end for David; and this is not the end for us. What did David do when the child had died and no amount of fasting and praying would any longer bring the child back? He proceeded to do six things.

> *Then David got up from the ground. After he had washed, put on lotions and changed his clothes, he went into the house of the LORD and worshiped. Then he went to his own house, and at his request they served him food, and he ate.* **2 Samuel 12:20**

David **washed** and **anointed** himself. He **changed his clothes** and **went to the house of the Lord**. There, he **worshipped God**. David then returned home and **ate**. Maybe this is what some of us need to do. Tell me that we have never emerged from a shower, feeling like a new human being? Do you suppose that may be how David felt; washing off the past and stepping out refreshed and set for a new beginning? That is what happens when we receive forgiveness; washed in the blood of the Lamb! I am sure that we can each recall a time when we drizzled oil upon our skin after a shower or bath, only to experience being exhilarated and revitalized as a new man or a new woman as a result? Our spirit within may have also felt energized and strengthened as a result. There is life in the anointing oil of the Holy Spirit and the Word of God.

Have there been days wherein we may have been in the doldrums? Not wanting to face the world, did we remain in our sweats for days on end? How did we feel after we finally took a shower, applied some oil or lotion, and arrayed ourselves in some articles of freshly cleaned clothing; or better yet, crawled into clean, crisp sheets? Were we not soothed and comforted? This process refreshed us physically, mentally, emotionally and yes, spiritually; getting us out of our melancholies and **condemnation**.

> **..., Yea, I have loved thee with an everlasting love: therefore with loving kindness have I drawn thee. Jeremiah 31:3 KJV**

And there is nothing better for a broken spirit then to fall on one's face before our Healer, our Sustainer, and our LOVE; feeding our spirit in the presence of our Maker. And as when any fast comes to an end, David rejuvenated himself by taking physical nourishment for his body. By these actions, David not only attended to his physical needs for nourishment, but focused on his emotional and spiritual needs as well, vital when accepting and receiving forgiveness; recharged for restoration.

> [26] **"So do not be afraid of them, for there is nothing concealed that will not be disclosed, or hidden that will not be made known ... [31] So don't be afraid; you are worth more than many sparrows. Matthew 10:26, 31**

We need to confess that we **Abandoned by Abortion**, once and for all! Shall we let our self-persecution and the enemy's **condemnation**s keep us from being about our Father's business; fulfilling our divinely appointed purpose? **Receive** God's forgiveness and let us **forgive ourselves**. Just as our God remembers our confessed sins **no more**, we must forget our sins and the sins of others. Why; because like David, it will not be possible to be **anointed,** and to be **healed**, and to **receive** His **Abundance**, should we continue to harbor such burdens of **condemnation** and destruction.

> *Though the mountains be shaken and the hills be removed, yet my unfailing love for you will not be shaken nor my covenant of peace be removed," says the* LORD, *who has compassion on you.* **Isaiah 54:10**

Today, many of us need to get out of the stagnations of our reality and become refreshed; physically, mentally, emotionally and spiritually renewed. Our sin is in the past; **remembered no more**. As David said:

> *But now that he is dead, why should I go on fasting? Can I bring him back again? I will go to him, but he will not return to me."* **2 Samuel 12: 23**

Forgiveness, healing and restoration, believe it or not, run on a two way street. God is more than enthusiastically eager and willing to do his part. However, we will have to be willing to do our part also. What is our part? Our part requires us to forgive ourselves, forgive others, and to be obedient and submit to our Healer. If we are to receive our healing, we will need to continuously apply His Healing Balm of Gilead through the renewal our minds; meditating on His Word, day and night. Our Restorer cannot do this part for us. That will require us to **choose** to free ourselves from the **condemnation** of **Abandoned by Abortion** and receive God's **abundance**; **Abandoned into Abundance**.

> *Forgive us our sins,* for we also *forgive everyone who sins against us*[a] ... **Luke 11:4**

> ... *thou shalt love thy neighbour as thyself.* **Matthew 22:39 KJV**

If we do not know how to love and forgive ourselves, then how are we going to be able to understand how to love and forgive our neighbors? Through our repentances and His restorations, God has an ***abundance*** awaiting each of our lives; if we but ***receive*** His forgiveness and walk in His divine purpose. We are here to accomplish **His will to be**

on earth as it is in heaven. Should we continue wickedness of our *"**little secrets**"*, like David, maligning God's good Name? Shall we be stripped of God's power and prevented from fulfilling our assigned mission?

But for God! As God washed away all of David's sins, He will wipe away our tears of grief, ***condemnation*** and repentance. He will even cleanse us of those atrocities that in the closeness of our past fellowship with Him, we never imagined inflicting on Jesus at the cross. He will purify us. Do we desire to be ***Abandoned into Abundance*** or to remain under the ***condemnation*** associated with our ***choice*** of ***Abandoned by Abortion***? ***But for God***; He knew! Omniscient, omnipotent, omnipresent God knew. ***ALL*** things work together for good for ***His will to be done on earth as it is in heaven***. Nothing will separate us from His love and He has promised to never leave or forsake us; never ***Abandoned by God***.

> ³⁸ For I am persuaded, that *neither death, nor life, nor angels, nor principalities, nor powers, nor things present, nor things to come,* ³⁹ *nor height, nor depth, nor any other creature, shall be able to separate us from the love of God, which is in Christ Jesus our Lord.* **Romans 8:38-39 KJV**
>
> *... because God has said, "Never will I leave you; never will I forsake you."*[a] **Hebrews 13:5b**
>
> *... And surely I am with you always, to the very end of the age.* **Matthew 28:20b**

8   ABANDONED BY SELF

> *Why my soul, are you downcast? Why so disturbed within me? Put your hope in God, for I will yet praise him, my Savior and my God..* **Psalm 42:11**

Have we just given up; now even **Abandoned by Self**? I would have to say that we might call David's condition as expressed above in Psalm 42 of the Old Testament, more than a little depressed. He was definitely in anguish; significantly **Abandoned by Self**. Have our failures caused us to abandon our **Faith**, and the achievement of our God given visions? Are we **choosing**, yes, I said **choosing**, to permit ourselves to be destroyed; consenting to the trickery of the enemy and the working of our own impatience to inhibit us from fulfilling God's calling for each of our respective lives?

> *² My soul thirsts for God, for the living God. When can I go and meet with God? ³ My tears have been my food day and night, while people say to me all day long, "Where is your God?" ⁴ These things I remember as I pour out my soul: how I used to go to the house of God under the protection of the Mighty One[a] with shouts of joy and praise among the festive throng. ⁵ Why, my soul, are you downcast? Why so disturbed within me? Put your hope in God, for I will yet praise him, my Savior and my God. ⁶ My soul is downcast within me; therefore I will remember you ... ⁷ Deep calls to deep in the roar of your waterfalls; all your waves and breakers have swept over me.* **Psalm 42:2-7**

We have a free will! Have our **choices** caused us to abandon **Hope**; hence causing us to be **Abandoned by Self**? Are we relinquishing the power of God and trading that power in for the damaging, destructive, disparaging lies of the devil? Is it possible that we are now ultimately surrendering to the denigrations of our lack of self-worth and becoming **Abandoned by Self**? Have we **chosen** to forsake each of our divinely ordained purposes?

> *For His anger lasts only a moment, but his favor lasts a lifetime; weeping may stay for the night, but rejoicing comes in the morning.* **Psalm 30:5**

Let us consider David's contemplation further. As with David, many of us today necessitate the mercy of God to deliver us out of the despondencies and dejections of our melancholies. In our hopelessness, we may be unaware that we are the ones that must take the first step. A decision must be made; a **choice** will be required. When we finally come to the end of ourselves, the end of our rope, and begin to long for the healing anointing found in God's Word, the doors of our gloominess cages will begin to crack open. It will be then and only then, that the healing balm of God's Word will be able to commence refreshing and restoring us physically, mentally, emotionally and spiritually.

> *[8] By day the LORD directs his love, at night his song is with me— a prayer to the God of my life. [9] I say to God my Rock, "Why have you forgotten me? Why must I go about mourning, oppressed by the enemy?" [10] My bones suffer mortal agony as my foes taunt me, saying to me all day long, "Where is your God?"* **Psalm 42:8-10**

In spite of the present blurry vision, activated by our many tears of abandonment, bitterness, discouragement, regret, sorrow, and lack of forgiveness, Jesus will still, if we **choose**, lead the way with His loving kindness. Jesus will hold our hands and guide our path to accomplish **His will to be done on earth as it is in heaven**.

> *I am the way, the truth, and the life: no man cometh unto the Father, but by me.* **John 14:6 KJV**

We need only wait and trust and ***hope*** in Him; not leaning on our own understanding but rather surrendering in trust to fulfill ***His kingdom come***.

> *⁵ Trust in the Lord with all thine heart; and lean not unto thine own understanding. ⁶ In all thy ways acknowledge him, and he shall direct thy paths.* **Proverbs 3:5-6 KJV**

We can ***choose*** to see the best in all because God through the blood of Jesus sees the best in all of us. He is our Blessed Assurance in and through our blessed spiritual status; our Anchor in the storm. Jesus is the solid, unchanging Rock, and with Him as our Truth, our Anchor, and our Stronghold, we need no longer focus on the gloom and doom wherein we may have ***chosen*** to be ***Abandoned by Self***.

> *The LORD is my rock, my fortress and my deliverer; my God is my rock, in whom I take refuge. He is my shield and the horn of my salvation, my stronghold.* **Psalm 18:2 KJV**

That may be easier said than done, we may ponder. David spent endless hours forlorn in misery, and yet, he also spent gratuitous hours in praise and worship; ever falling more in ***Love*** with his God. Such a contradiction; how was this possible? Remember, all things are possible with God!

> **With men this is impossible; *but* WITH GOD ALL THINGS ARE POSSIBLE.** **Matthew 19:26 KJV**

All things are possible if we ***choose*** to brandish the spoken Sword of the powerful and eternal Word of God. There are an ***abundance*** of words being spoken today that are not the Word of God: the news, the radio, the TV, the neighbor, our friend. More than likely, those words are not God's Words. What words are spewing forth out of our disheartened little mouths at the present time or maybe, for the last ten years of our despondency? Are we aware that there is death and life in the power of our tongues? Have the relevance and declaration of our words set us to be ***Abandoned by Self***?

> ***Death and life are in the power of the tongue: and they that love it shall eat the fruit thereof.*** **Psalm 18:21 KJV**

In Genesis 1 of the Old Testament, God spoke and created life: sun, moon, stars, water, land, birds, fish, animals, man, etc. We have seen people or heard of people that talk to their plants. Some would say that talking to the plants speaks life into them! What would happen if we attempted to only speak God's Words, or at least paraphrased God's Words in our communication today? Would we be speaking life into our self; no longer being ***Abandoned by Self***?

> ***So then faith cometh by hearing, and hearing by the word of God.*** **Romans 10:17 KJV**

No matter where we are or where we go these days, it is often challenging not to hear the words that people natter to each other: parents to children, spouse to spouse, political opponents, sports rivals or TV announcers. Are they always speaking life into each other by what they are uttering or, are they killing each other with their verbiage? Are they audibly sucking the last breath of life out of someone's dreams, hopes or goals; words that could potentially cause that someone to also be ***Abandoned by Self***?

God's ***Hope*** for us is to speak His Word. His will is for us to speak life into ourselves and others by declaring His healing Word. His Word is the Sword of the Spirit. It is designed to empower us to deflect the foils of the enemy that we may consciously or subconsciously **receive**. Such negative affirmation may cause us to ultimately descend into a downward spiral of debilitation and ineffectiveness for service to the King of Kings; leaving us **Abandoned by Self**. Crippled by such assertions may restrict us from performing **God's will to be done on earth as it is in heaven**. It is imperative that we study, practice and master the application of His Sword. God told Ezekiel to literally eat the scroll that contained His Word; God wills that we each literally hunger for Him and His Word.

> *¹ ... And he said to me, "Son of man, eat what is before you, eat this scroll; then go and speak to the people of Israel." ² So I opened my mouth, and he gave me the scroll to eat. ³ Then he said to me, "Son of man, eat this scroll I am giving you and fill your stomach with it." So I ate it, and it tasted as sweet as honey in my mouth.* **Ezekiel 3:1-3**

Even Jesus said that man shall not live by bread alone:

> *... Man shall not live by bread alone, but by every word that proceedeth out of the mouth of God.* **Matthew 4:4 KJV**

Did you catch that? "**Out of the mouth of God**" must mean the spoken Word of God; the spoken Word that created heaven and earth and everything in between. We have the Word of God to place in our bellies, to place in our minds, to place in our mouths; and like the Sword of the Spirit, to place in the hands of the believer. Now, it is up to each of us to **choose** to do with it what we may. Like a warrior, it is essential that we practice reciting the Word ahead of time; anticipating, preparing and rehearsing to utilize it in each specific situation as it arises in our life.

Will we be attuned to the Holy Spirit and to the Word of God? Have we been primed to instantly recall which thrust, which position best suits the precise moment; hearing God's Spirit, His Word, and His instructions, hidden in our hearts? Practice, Practice, Practice!

David praised God in the midst of his storm; his battle with downheartedness and despair. The facts around his circumstances had not change, but he made a ***choice***, an act of the will, to praise God in the midst of his tempest. There is power, healing power, in praising and in adoring and in worshipping and in hearing the spoken Word of God.

> *The Lord is my strength and my shield; my heart trusted in Him, and I am helped: therefore my heart greatly rejoiceth; and with my song will I praise him.* **Psalm 28:7 KJV**

Many years have passed on my journey to joy. It has only been in recent years that I can now articulate my current understanding of true ***gratitude*** and joy. The Biblical meaning of and my actual receiving of the Fruit of the Spirit seed of joy as affectionately planted in my heart's garden by Jesus sprung forth with ***gratitude***. Guilt and condemnation are only to be followed by depression and unhappiness. As I have said before, forgiveness from God is one of the first freedom steps in the healing process. The resulting release of joy, erupting through this healing progression, is just one of the many blessings provided to each of us by the Holy Spirit in our respective Fruit of the Spirit heart's gardens.

> *... the voice of them that shall say, praise the Lord of hosts: for the Lord is good; for his mercy endureth for ever: and of them that shall bring the sacrifice of praise into the house of the Lord ...* **Jeremiah 33:11 KJV**

And so in my brokenness, the Master began melting and molding this new creature. And as repeated from before, in that development was birthed my **Gratitude Book**. Every evening before going to sleep, I would recall and journal the many events of the day. I had a **choice**. Was I going to focus on the negative or was I going to rejoice in the positive blessings as I trusted in my Jesus? When we strip away all the glittering blinders and actually experience the reality of the many blessings taken for granted in this great country, we begin to not only witness, but hail with exultant joy, the bountiful provisions of God. Yes, we have clean water to drink, to bath and to swim. We have food in our belly, and many of us have our health. We hear, smell, see and walk; and maybe some of us can still run!

> *You make known to me the path of life; you will fill me with joy in your presence, with eternal pleasures at your right hand.* **Psalm 16:11**

Purposing to concentrate on my many blessings, I would ignore the diverse false accusations and guilty **condemnations** from Satan as related to my family or anything or anyone else. My Jesus had forgiven me. I was learning to receive and give forgiveness. I had asked my adult children for forgiveness. The acts of giving forgiveness to me and receiving forgiveness from Him were now between them and Almighty God.

In spite of what is about me, I am forgiven and, I have forgiven myself. Like David, I was rising above in adoring **gratitude** and praise; released from within would rise the spirit of joy and song. By simply adjusting my focus, I purpose to rejoice in and over the simple, uncomplicated matters of life.

> [22] *and ye now therefore have sorrow: but I will see you again, and your heart shall rejoice, and your joy no man taketh from you.* [23] *and in that day ye*

> *shall ask me nothing. Verily, verily, I say unto you, whatsoever ye shall ask the Father in my name, He will give it you.* ²⁴ *Hitherto have ye asked nothing in my name: ask, and ye shall receive, that your joy may be full.* **John 16:22-24 KJV**

Yes, we may now have sorrow in this disaster that has caused us to be ***Abandoned by Self***. However, by the divine revelation found in God's Word and in the power of praise, and worship and adoration with ***gratitude***, we may now ***choose*** to praise and rejoice in our Jesus! By obeying and following His directions, we may gratefully learn to ***Love*** and to trust Him during this season and always; no matter what storms may befall us. His Light will appear at the end of the tunnel. By concentrating on the positive of His promises found in His Word and not being enticed by the cage of negative lies from the gates of hell, these same promises will change every aspect of our lives.

> *Whom having not seen, ye love; in whom, though now ye see him not, yet believing, ye rejoice with joy unspeakable and full of glory*: **1 Peter 1:8 KJV**

The changes will probably appear more from within than from without. They will most definitely not transpire within our pre-prescribed time frames. However, He tells us to ask, and the answer will come; and we will rejoice! How does one have exultant joy and rejoice when everything that is most dear to them is being stripped away or never existed? The answer again is ***gratitude*** and praise. And as my historic measurement of lack decreased, my divine measurement of ***abundance*** increased; rooted in ***gratitude*** to produce the fruit of joy.

Through the Word of Truth, I pray that we make the ***choice*** to no longer accept invitations to depressing, melancholy and self-condemnation parties. But rather, I pray that we each ***choose*** to receive the ***abundance*** awaiting each of us at Christian optimism parties *ONLY*! Let us attend gatherings wherein God reminds us that He, and only He, is omniscient. Satan is *NOT*! Satan may put the thoughts in our head, but we are not required to entertain them within wherein Christ resides.

> *...CHRIST IN YOU, THE HOPE OF GLORY*: Colossians 1:27 KJV

Let us speak His Word *OUT LOUD* no matter the number of guest we may be entertaining; even if we are the only one in attendance. Let us no longer be *Abandoned by Self*; Christ in us, our hope of glory! After all, didn't God speak, and the world and all of its glory were created? Didn't Jesus speak specific Scriptural truths to oppose specific satanic inaccuracies when He was tempted in the wilderness? Didn't Jesus rebuke Peter who, like some of our friends and family today, was used as a channel from Satan? And when the devil and his many minions are plaguing us with false accusations such as guilt, lies, depression, lustful thoughts, etc., etc., etc., should we not be *AUDIBLY* rebuking him, and not succumbing to being *Abandoned by Self*?

> *... he rebuked Peter, saying, Get thee behind me, Satan: for thou savourest not the things that be of God, but the things that be of men.* Mark 8:33 KJV

Have we ever considered that when we pray God's Holy Word back to Him, or we speak it in our daily lives in an affirmation to ourselves or in encouragement to another that our words, His Word, is carried off, and continues about throughout eternity? The Word of God is *ETERNAL*. Spoken, it affirms *His will be done*!

> *[10] ... as the rain cometh down, and the snow from heaven, and returneth not thither, but watereth the earth, and maketh it bring forth and bud, that it may give seed to the sower, and bread to the*

> *eater:* ⁱⁱ *So shall my word be that goeth forth out of my mouth: It Shall Not Return Unto Me Void, But It Shall Accomplish That Which I Please, And It Shall Prosper In The Thing Whereto I Sent It.* **Isaiah 55:10-11 KJV**

I do not know the work God was performing in David's heart during this period of melancholy. Possibly he had sinned, or perhaps he was "*self*" focused for a period of time. Then again, God was conceivably breaking, melting and molding him further. Whatever the course of those events, David finally began to praise God in spite of his circumstances. Whatever the purpose for this refining, God's Word says that there is a price to pay for lack of ***gratitude*** for all of God's many myriads of blessings.

> ⁴⁷ *Because you did not serve the LORD your God joyfully and gladly in the time of prosperity,* ⁴⁸ *therefore in hunger and thirst, in nakedness and dire poverty, you will serve the enemies the LORD sends against you. He will put an iron yoke on your neck until he has destroyed you.* **Deuteronomy 28:47-48**

Has our lack of ***gratitude***, our focus on "*self*", and not God's will for our lives, and our longing for things, wants verses needs, put a yoke of iron upon our necks; a yoke that in our despair has caused us to be ***Abandoned by Self***? Who do we want to serve; the Lord with gladness and ***gratitude*** or, to be imprisoned by the tormenter? Do we desire to be ***Abandoned into Abundance*** or to remain ***Abandoned by Self***? Let me repeat, His Word declares that there is never a joyful outcome when rebellion and lack of gratitude are present.

> *I tell you that in the same way there will be more rejoicing in heaven over one sinner who repents than over ninety-nine righteous persons who do not need to repent.* **Luke 15:7**

What is the message of the spoken Word of God to those ***Abandoned by Self***? The significance is the unyielding healing power of God's spoken Word to empower us to no longer be ***Abandoned by Self***, but rather, to arise in praise and adoration and ***gratitude*** of our most high God. God's Word conveys to us that there is life or death in the power of the tongue. Are we going to be ***defeated***, ***Abandoned by Self***, or ***victorious*** in His ***abundance***; ***Never Abandoned by God***?

Do we desire to be ***Abandoned into Abundance*** or to remain ***Abandoned by Self***? What are we going to listen to; what are we going to say; what are we going to pray? Let us take the Word of God and hide it in our hearts; meditating on it, renewing our minds with it, and professing and proclaiming it. In ***gratitude***, let us live ***abundant*** victorious Christian lives for the entire world to see; for all the world to see Christ in us, our ***Hope*** of glory. ***His will be done on earth as it is in heaven***. We are His ***Chosen*** and He has promised never to leave us and never to forsake us; never ***Abandoned by God***.

> *Ye have not chosen me, but I have chosen you, and ordained you, that ye should go and bring forth fruit, and that your fruit should remain …* **John 15:16 KJV**
>
> *… because God has said, "Never will I leave you; never will I forsake you."*[a] **Hebrews 13:5b**
>
> *… And surely I am with you always, to the very end of the age.* **Matthew 28:20b**

9 ABANDONED BY OUR CHILDREN

> [10] *Hope deferred maketh the heart sick: but when the desire cometh, it is a tree of life ...* [19] *the desire accomplished is sweet to the soul ...* **Proverbs 13:12, 19 KJV**

Visiting the local nursing home or even those in my Florida neighborhood, I sometimes encounter individuals who are, as we may now be also, ***Abandoned by our Children***. Having already travelled countless miles on life's perilous journey, they either, through each of their own faults or through no fault of their own, and like some of us today, have been ***Abandoned by our Children***. Although I initially attempted to be a perfect parent when first coddling my little brood, I soon came to realize that there is not a perfect parent that walks the face of this earth. Jesus was the only perfect person to tread this track. Because many of us have not marched this parent passageway before, we will make, do make, and have made mistakes.

Even after becoming a child of God and purposing to make Jesus, Lord of our lives, we still frequently stumble and fall on this parental pathway. As a result of any number of our imperfections, we may be ***Abandoned by our Children***. For my children who are now adults, I know that the subsequent reality of the perfect Christian life that protected their peaceable surroundings was splintered by the cruel realities of our family's divorce. The seeds of that calamity have been fertilized with the pain of ponder to such an extent that those seeds have since sprouted forth a harvest of bitterness, judgment, rejection, and lack of forgiveness. Like so many others for greater or lesser reasons, we are ***Abandoned by our Children***.

> *⁹ Cast me not off in the time of old age; forsake me not when my strength faileth. ¹⁰ For mine enemies speak against me; and they that lay wait for my soul take counsel together ... ¹² O God, be not far from me: O my God, make haste for my help. ¹³ Let them be confounded and consumed that are adversaries to my soul; let them be covered with reproach and dishonour that seek my hurt ... ¹⁸ Now also when I am old and grey headed, O God, FORSAKE ME NOT; UNTIL I HAVE SHEWED THY STRENGTH UNTO THIS GENERATION, AND THY POWER TO EVERYONE THAT IS TO COME.*
> Psalm 71:9-10, 12-13, 18 KJV

Although David had a heart for God and was loved by Him, he was a terrible parent, as depicted throughout 2 Samuel 13-20 in the Old Testament. In Psalm 71 above, we once again witness David's heart lamenting. This time, his lament is over the disarray of his home. David, in his old age, is seeking God's wisdom and protection. He has too many wives and too many undisciplined sons. Most of his sons, as may be the case in some of our lives, were not too thrilled with their father or mother. Maybe they, like some of our offspring, were not given their heart's desire whilst in our care, or later. Or, possibly they were, and are still, ungratefully seeking more.

David's first wife was Saul's second daughter, Michal. Initially promised to David in marriage before David left for battle, Saul gave her to someone else in his absence. Eventually, she was returned to David. However, on his run from Saul and before her return, David acquired two wives, Ahinoam and Abigail. Settling in Hebron, his first son Amnon was born to Ahinoam, his first wife. Soon, his second son Daniel was born to Abigail, his second wife.

David reigned as king at Hebron for seven years and six months. There, David acquired a few more wives, and six more sons were born to him. His third son Absalom was born to Maachah; his fourth son Adonijah was born to

Haggith; his fifth, son Shephatiah was born to Abital; and his sixth son, Ithream was born to Eglah. Six sons would be a handful on their own, but combine that with just as many wives, his continuous absence in the many wars of the land, and the demands of his kingly responsibility; no wonder his house was in upheaval. David was being pulled in so many directions, and some of those demands were not given the attention they required. Reminds me a bit of the demands placed on so many of our parson's today wherein their personal families are often abandoned; becoming the ones that must endure their many absences.

If that bit of pandemonium was not enough, over the next thirty three year reign, after David arrived as king in Jerusalem, he took on even more wives and concubines. And to follow that, was the birthing of even more sons and a daughter. Of Bathsheba, remember Uriah's wife, four sons were born: Shimea, Shobab, Nathan, and Solomon. From his other wives were birthed Ibhar, Elishama, Eliphelet, Nogah, Nepheg, Japhia, Elishama, Eliada, and Eliphelet. This list does not include the sons of his concubines, and his daughter, Tamar. Combined with his six sons born in Hebron, I can imagine the boys being quite the handful of commotion bordering on anarchy; never mind the feat of juggling those many wives!

Absalom, David's third son had a sister named Tamar. She was raped by Amnon, David's first born son. When Absalom became aware of this atrocity, he took his disgraced sister to live in his home. She remained there, dishonored and desolate. When David heard of the rape, he was greatly grieved, but took no action. Absalom hated his brother for this evil, but took a page from his father's book; doing nothing at the time except to refuse to talk to him. However, unlike his father, and two years later, Absalom invited his father David and all the king's sons, his brothers, to join him for a great feast. Absalom's sheepshearers had just finished in the fields. David declined the invitation but sent the rest of his boys off to enjoy the celebration. Absalom had established a plan. His servants were to kill his oldest brother Amnon when his heart was merry with wine. Remember, this was the brother that raped Tamar. When Absalom's servants had killed him, all the king's sons fled the feast and scattered in safeguard of their lives.

David was initially informed that Absalom had slain all of his sons. On hearing such, David arose, tore his garments, and lay on the ground in mourning. All of his servants stood by with their clothes rent also. However, David's brother soon arrived and clarified that not all of his sons had been slain, just Amnon. As soon as he had finished speaking, all of David's sons arrived safe after their escape from the banquet. They too wept in grief. However, Absalom had fled. In spite of what Amnon had done to Tamar and the disgrace that she was enduring in her life, David still mourned for his rapist first born every day.

Absalom spent the next three years in exile. Overcoming his grief for Amnon, David now longed to see Absalom. Joab, David's military leader, perceived that David yearned to see Absalom. He therefore sought Absalom and brought him back to Jerusalem. David told Joab that Absalom could return to his own house, but he would never see David's face. Absalom dwelt there two full years, never seeing his father's face. Eventually, Absalom requested an audience with Joab to arrange for him to see his father. Joab would not respond. In his frustration, Absalom had his servants set Joab's fields on fire. Joab then went to David and told him that Absalom longed to see him. Absalom was allowed to come into the king presence, bowing before him with his face to the ground. David kissed him, but Absalom returned home, never really seeing his father's face.

In his pride, Absalom arrogantly acquired chariots and horses, with fifty men to run before him. He began to rise early and stand at the city gate. When any man had a controversy and came to the king for judgment, Absalom, challenging his father's leadership and authority, would hear and rule on the matter. Desiring that he were made judge in the land, Absalom began to steal the hearts of the men of Israel. He aspired to carry out justice! Finally leaving for Hebron wherein David was first king, Absalom dispatched spies throughout all the tribes of Israel, rallying an uprising against his father David. For those Israelites that would, they were to declare him king of Israel in Hebron upon hearing the sound of his trumpet.

David received a message advising him that the hearts of the men of Israel were now favoring Absalom. Fearing a pending attack on Jerusalem, David gathered his servants and his troops, and fled to a place that was a safe distance away. Absalom, as king of Israel, advanced to Jerusalem to reign as King of Judah as well. Exiled, David advised all those he encountered that his son Absalom sought to take his life. He was **Abandoned by his Children**. In further rebellion and usurping the king's authority in Jerusalem, it became known throughout Israel that Absalom had done the unthinkable. He had relations with David's concubines.

The courageous warriors of Judah who honored God went out in battle against Israel. Through the power of God, the armies of David slaughtered twenty thousand men of Israel that day. When Absalom met the servants of David, he fled. Riding a mule into the wooded areas, his thick matted locks became entangled in the bulky substantial limbs of a great oak tree. The mule that was under him vanished and he was left dangling from the branches. It is there that he is killed by Joab, David's military leader. Joab cast his body into a great pit in the woods, and laid stones atop that. With their new leader dead, all Israel fled to their homes that day.

¹ In thee, O Lord, do I put my trust: let me never be put to confusion. ² Deliver me in thy righteousness, and cause me to escape: incline thine ear unto me, and save me. ³ Be thou my strong habitation, whereunto I may continually resort: thou hast given commandment to save me; for thou art my rock and my fortress. ⁴ Deliver me, O my God, out of the hand of the wicked, out of the hand of the unrighteous and cruel man. ⁵ For thou art my hope, O Lord God: thou art my trust from my youth. ⁶ By thee have I been holden up from the womb: thou art he that took me out of my mother's bowels: my praise shall be continually of thee. ⁷ I am as a wonder unto many; but thou art my strong refuge. ⁸ Let my mouth be filled with thy praise and with thy honour all the day. **Psalm 71:1-8 KJV**

Then Adonijah, David's fourth son next to Absalom, declared that he, and not Solomon, should be king after their father. David had never disciplined or shown displeasure for any of his sons' behaviors. In other words, David was not a good disciplinarian and tended to spoil his children. At another great slewing feast of sheep, oxen and fatten cattle, Adonijah invited his brothers and all the king's servants of Judah. He desired that they declare him king, and not Solomon. There was poor old David, on his death bed and, like some of us may be today, on the brink of a potential uprising; being **Abandoned by our Children**!

However, he did not invite his father David, the prophet Nathan, or his brother Solomon. When Adonijah's plans became known to Nathan and Bathsheba, they quickly addressed the matter with King David. Upon hearing of the attempt to empower Adonijah king over Solomon, David proclaimed that as the Lord lives and has redeemed his soul, and by the Lord God of Israel, Solomon shall reign after him. Solomon shall sit upon his throne in his stead. As such, Nathan proceeded to anoint Solomon king. When they blew the trumpet, and shouted "**God save King Solomon**", Adonijah and his guests, on hearing the clamor in the distance, hastily finished their meal and scattered.

Adonijah feared Solomon who was now anointed king. He fled for the protection of the horns of the altar. Advised of Adonijah anxious actions, Solomon declared that if his brother presented himself as a worthy man, then he would not have anything to be frightened; Solomon would not harm him. However, if there was wickedness in his activities, then he would die. So King Solomon sent, and Adonijah was brought down from the altar. He bowed before his brother King Solomon. Eventually, Adonijah was put to death by Solomon for his evil intentions.

In this brief dissertation of just some of the exploits of David's sons, we may identify why he, in his old age, was calling on the name of the Lord for help, deliverance, protection and wisdom. Like many parents today, he had executed many mistakes in his family's lives. One son had raped his sister; another son killed that rapist brother. That same son tried to dethrone and kill his father. A third son tried to usurp the anointing of his brother as successor to his father's throne. And now, David was failing on his death bed. Although not the same set of circumstances, it is not uncommon for many of us to have also claimed these very Scriptures in the torrents of judgment, coveting, desertion, disregard, neglect, rejection, and usurping, enacted against us; ***Abandoned by our Children***.

> *[10] For mine enemies speak against me; and they that lay wait for my soul take counsel together, [11] Saying, God hath forsaken him: persecute and take him; for there is none to deliver him ... [14] But I will hope continually, and will yet praise thee more and more. [15] My mouth shall shew forth thy righteousness and thy salvation all the day; for I know not the numbers thereof. [16] I will go in the*

> *strength of the Lord God: I will make mention of thy righteousness ...* **Psalm 71:10-11, 14-16 KJV**

But for God Who sent His Son Jesus to wash away ***All*** of our sins and has removed them ***ALL*** away, "*as far as the east is from the west to remember no more*". Purposing to concentrate on our many blessings, we can ***choose*** to no longer live under Satan's diverse false or "*true*" accusations and guilty ***condemnations*** as related to our failings, our family or anything or anyone else. Possibly we did the best we could do. We are not perfect, but no more ***condemnation***!

> *As far as the east is from the west, so far hath he removed our transgressions from us.* **Psalm 103:12 KJV**

> *having canceled the charge of our legal indebtedness, which stood against us and condemned us; he has taken it away, nailing it to the cross.* **Colossians 2:14**

> *Therefore, there is now NO CONDEMNATION for those who are in Christ Jesus.* **Romans 8:1** (Emphasis supplied)

If we have confessed our sins, then Jesus has forgiven us. We must ever learn to forgive ourselves. But first we must learn to love ourselves. If we cannot endeavor to love and forgive ourselves, then how can we love and forgive others as ourselves?

> *... thou shalt love thy neighbour as thyself.* **Matthew 22:39 KJV**

> *... love your enemies, bless them that curse you, do good to them that hate you, and pray for them which despitefully use you, and persecute you;* **Matthew 5:44 KJV**

As we learn to receive and give forgiveness, let us each ask our children, whether young or old, for forgiveness. The acts of giving and receiving forgiveness, hopefully from them, will be the fertilizer necessary to sprout the new seeds of agape love within our family's gardens' of life. Should they not be ready at this particular juncture to grant forgiveness, then we must commit them to God. Pray for them and wait for the fulfillment of God's will and His restoration in each of our lives. If we have done what is possible for us on our journey of healing forgiveness within our families, then it is now between them and Almighty God. Remember, He works within the realm of impossible.

> **And he said, The *THINGS* which are impossible with men *ARE POSSIBLE WITH GOD*. Luke 18:27 KJV**
>
> *and we know that in all things God works for the good of those who love him, who[a] have been called according to his purpose.* **Romans 8:28**
>
> *Now faith is confidence in what we hope for and assurance about what we do not see.* **Hebrews 11:1**

Yes, all things work together for good to them that love God, to those who are the called according to His purpose. But maybe that promise is not currently visible in our present reality. Is that not what faith is, believing in something that God has promised even though we may not presently be able to see it? He works ALL things to His purpose for **His will to be done, one earth as it is in heaven**. Shall we pull up our boot straps, and step forward, pressing on? Shall we forget what is behind as God has forgotten and removed *"as far as the east is from the west"*? For now, let us arise in faith, and in adoring **gratitude** and praise in sincere acceptance; releasing God's immeasurable joy from within as David patterned to us.

¹⁷ O God, thou hast taught me from my youth: and hitherto have I declared thy wondrous works. ¹⁸ Now also when I am old and grey headed, O God, forsake me not; until I have shewed thy strength unto this generation, and thy power to everyone that is to come. ¹⁹ Thy righteousness also, O God, is very high, who hast done great things: O God, who is like unto thee! ²⁰ Thou, which hast shewed me great and sore troubles, shalt quicken me again, and shalt bring me up again from the depths of the earth. ²¹ Thou shalt increase my greatness, and comfort me on every side. ²² I will also praise thee with the psaltery, even thy truth, O my God: unto thee will I sing with the harp, O thou Holy One of Israel. ²³ My lips shall greatly rejoice when I sing unto thee; and my soul, which thou hast redeemed. ²⁴ My tongue also shall talk of thy righteousness all the day long: for they are confounded, for they are brought unto shame, that seek my hurt. **Psalm 71:17-24 KJV**

As we await the power of God's outstretched hand to fashion His will in our adult children's hearts, let us each adjust our focus, and set our positions on performing ***His will be done on earth as it is in heaven***! Let us purpose to rejoice in and over the simple, uncomplicated matters of life. Let us catch sight of those that are placed in our daily paths; divine appointments to fulfill His purpose. It is amazing what bounty our Jesus truly lays before each of us when we endeavor to fix our sights on Him. Refusing to travel down ***Condemnation Lane***, we steady our course on our positive blessings. Forgetting what is behind, what had to be broken to get us to this place on His path, we become new! ***We press on***!

> *¹² NOT THAT I HAVE ALREADY ATTAINED, or am already perfected; <u>BUT I PRESS ON</u> ... ¹³ ... I do not count myself to have apprehended; but one thing I do, FORGETTING THOSE THINGS WHICH*

ARE BEHIND AND REACHING FORWARD TO THOSE THINGS WHICH ARE AHEAD, ¹⁴ I PRESS TOWARD THE GOAL for the prize of the upward call of God in CHRIST JESUS. **Philippians 3:12-14 KJV**

In the midst of a potentially perplexing journey, let us leave the rubbish behind and press on to do **His will be done on earth as it is in heaven**. God is in control, and by faith, we may begin to see His miracle of restoration in each of our lives. Do we desire to be **Abandoned into Abundance** or to remain in the misery of being **Abandoned by our Children**?

> *¹⁰ Hope deferred maketh the heart sick: but when the desire cometh, it is a tree of life ... ¹⁹ The desire accomplished is sweet to the soul ...* **Proverbs 13:12, 19 KJV**

Should we not see the fulfillment of God's healing balm of Gilead within our respective families on our earthly sojourn, we may still accomplish His purpose for **His will to be done**. We have a **choice**! We can hence forward allow **His kingdom come on earth** through the expression of Who He is through us to a broken and hurting world that surrounds us. Our journey's pain may be just the tools the Master has bestowed on us to perform that task in expressing His love. Let us thank our Father for His love and for never giving up on us; for His promise to never leave or forsake us. We are NEVER **Abandoned by God**.

> *... because God has said, "Never will I leave you; never will I forsake you."*[a] **Hebrews 13:5b**
>
> *... And surely I am with you always, to the very end of the age.* **Matthew 28:20b**

CONCLUSION - NEVER ABANDONED BY GOD

> *... Yea, I have loved thee with an everlasting love: therefore with loving kindness have I drawn thee.* Jeremiah 31:3 KJV

> *...I will restore to you the years that the locust hath eaten ... which I sent among you.* Joel 2:25 KJV

But for God! Whether we believed that we were Abandoned at Conception, Abandoned in Adolescence, Marriage, or Divorce, or possibly even Abandoned by our Church, we are **never Abandoned by God**. In desperation and upheaval, we may have Abandoned our Children, Abandoned by Abortion, Abandoned Self, or been Abandoned by our Children, but we were and are ***Never Abandoned by God***. God knows the plans that He has for us; ***His will to be done on earth as it is in heaven***!

> *[11] For I know the thoughts that I think toward you, saith the Lord, thoughts of peace, and not of evil, to give you an expected end. [12] Then shall ye call upon me, and ye shall go and pray unto me, and I will hearken unto you. [13] And ye shall seek me, and find me, when ye shall search for me with all your heart. [14] And I will be found of you, saith the Lord: and I will turn away your captivity, and I will gather you from all the nations, and from all the places whither I have driven you, saith the Lord; and I will bring you again into the place whence I caused you to be carried away captive.* Jeremiah 29:11-14 KJV

Maybe we were ***abandoned*** through death, or any number of other forms of abandonment not discussed here. No matter the conditions of our respective desertion or relinquishment and the sins that may be encompassed therein, there is mercy, and there is forgiveness. Yes, the penalty for our sins is death. However because of God's redemptive plan, Jesus' sacrifice, the shedding of His blood at the cross, and because of God's individual plan for each of our lives, He offers us forgiveness and Salvation.

Joseph's life from adolescence to manhood was engraved with a purpose. His two sons were named Manasseh and Ephraim. Manasseh means "For God has made me forget all my toil, and all my father's house". Joseph had to put all the bitterness of his previous life's experiences behind him in order that he might press on; to step forward and to be released from his personal prison. His second son's name, Ephraim means "God has caused me to be fruitful in the land of my affliction". God blessed Joseph with **abundance** for giving and receiving forgiveness to his brothers and the lot that he endured. Because of God's breaking, melting and molding of his heart, Joseph was able to say to his brothers:

> *... ye thought evil against me; but GOD MEANT IT UNTO GOOD, to bring to pass, as it is this day, TO SAVE MUCH PEOPLE ALIVE.* **Genesis 50:20 KJV**

Are we too anointed and appointed *"to save much people alive"*? Who are the people that we are to introduce to our Lord and Savior; to be saved through their respective receipt of the Salvation provided by Jesus' shed blood on the cross? Like Joseph, what purpose **"God meant it unto good"** has He carved into each of our respective hearts as a result of our many trials of refinement? Shall we harvest the **abundance** of His fruit from the cultivation by His Spirit, as we accomplish **His will be done on earth as it is in heaven**; *"to save a people alive"*?

Has the mighty hand of God also placed us into a complex and unimaginable set of circumstances for the Salvation and purpose of even one soul; for this very moment of deliverance; "*for such a time as this*"? Have we been *chosen* for this purpose? Will another do it if we do not?

> *For if thou altogether holdest thy peace at this time, then shall ... deliverance arise ... from another place ... and who knoweth whether thou art come to the kingdom FOR SUCH A TIME AS THIS?* **Esther 4:14 KJV**
>
> **Ye have not chosen me, but *I HAVE CHOSEN YOU, and ORDAINED YOU*, that ye should *GO AND BRING FORTH FRUIT*, and that your fruit should remain ... John 15:16 KJV**

Before the beginning of time, God planned the work or purpose He had for us. We are His *anointed*; *set apart* for a purpose to bring *His will be done on earth as it is in heaven*. He began a good work in us. He will complete it.

> *Now know I that the Lord saveth his ANOINTED; he will hear him from his holy heaven with the saving strength of his right hand.* **Psalm 20:6 KJV**
>
> *But know that the Lord hath SET APART him that is godly for himself: the Lord will hear when I call unto him.* **Psalm 4:3 KJV**
>
> *Being confident of this very thing, that he which hath begun a good work in you will perform it until the day of Jesus Christ*: **Philippians 1:6 KJV**

If we have accepted Christ's payment on the cross for *ALL* of our sins, our iniquities of yesterday, today and tomorrow, and if we have confessed our wrongdoings to God, then He has forgiven us. Now, He only sees us as white as snow.

> *If we confess our sins, he is faithful and just to forgive us our sins, and to cleanse us from all unrighteousness.* **1 John 1:9 KJV**
>
> *... though your sins be as scarlet, they shall be as white as snow; though they are red like crimson, they shall be like wool.* **Isaiah 1:18**

If we have received this gift of forgiveness, blotting out ***ALL*** of our failings, then why do we continually go dumpster diving; retrieving the refuge of sin that has been removed *as far as the east is from the west* and remembered no more by God after our confessions? The debt has been paid; Jesus paid it ***ALL***! God no longer ***condemns*** us! Why do we continue to ***condemn*** ourselves?

> *Blotting out the handwriting of ordinances that was against us, which was contrary to us, and took it out of the way, nailing it to his cross;* **Colossians 2:14 KJV**
>
> *As far as the east is from the west, so far hath he removed our transgressions from us.* **Psalm 103:12 KJV**
>
> *Therefore, there is now NO CONDEMNATION for those who are in Christ Jesus.* **Romans 8:1** (Emphasis supplied)

But for God! Do we still think that we were ***Abandoned at Conception***? Who could have imagined this, ***His abundance created in us*** who were deposited into our mother's wombs? God does not make junk! We were not ***Abandoned at Conception*** for we are the sum of many of His precious thoughts. Shall we ***choose*** to doubt and remain delusional about being ***Abandoned at Conception*** or shall we ***choose*** to rise above; to be ***Abandoned into Abundance*** and ***Never Abandoned by God***!

> *⁷ How precious to me are your thoughts,[a] God! How vast is the sum of them! ¹⁸ Were I to count them, they would outnumber the grains of sand— when I awake, I am still with you.* **Psalm139:17-18**

But for God! Do we continue to trudge along in defeat because we believe we were ***Abandoned in Adolescence***? Have we or others forgotten ***His abundance created in us***? Like Joseph, we, like a vast number of forsaken teenagers with ever changing life's circumstances, are evolving in this world. Through the handiwork of God, the Master craftsman, we are being molded and empowered through our specific sets of conditions. Each being chisel and finely tuned for the great work of ***His abundance created in us***, we are the ***Chosen "for such a time as this"***, to go and bring forth fruit. Not ***Abandoned in Adolescence***, but rather ***Abandoned into Abundance***!

> *Ye have not chosen me, but I have chosen you ... that ye should go and bring forth fruit, and that your fruit should remain ...* **John 15:16 KJV**

But for God! Do we continue to focus on the fact that we may have been ***Abandoned in Marriage***? Through sin, people will disappoint and hurt us. However, Jesus, in His quest for an eternal love affair with us, will ever woo us with ***His abundance created in us***. Should we ***choose***, He will teach us how to love with His agape love, no matter the state of our earthly wed. We are the Bride of Christ, and Jesus is our Groom. Through the healing balm of His Word, His Spirit whispers into us, ***His abundance created in us***. He knows and has known us from the beginning of time. He made us. Our eternal Husband Jesus discloses to us that before we knew Him, before we committed our respective lives to Him, He has loved each of us, His Bride, with His everlasting agape love. Not ***Abandoned in Marriage***, but rather ***Abandoned into***

Abundance! Our Groom will hold our hands and walk with each of us, His Bride, as our eternal love. He will never leave or forsake us; never ***Abandoned in Marriage***!

> *... yea, I have loved thee with an everlasting love: therefore with loving kindness have I drawn thee.*
> **Jeremiah 31:3 KJV**

But for God! Are we ***choosing*** to remain angry at our Maker, because we have been rejected by this marriage breaker; ***Abandoned in Divorce***? If we have asked God for forgiveness then if we ***choose***, we may be freed from the bondage of the ***condemnation*** associated with such. God will teach us to receive His forgiveness. He will supply the grace and strength to receive forgiveness from others and to give forgiveness also. God will empower us to ask others for forgiveness and to forgive ourselves. By our actions, He is able to wipe our slates clean with the blood of our eternal Husband, Jesus; to release ***His abundance created in us***!

> ***FOR THY MAKER IS THINE HUSBAND***; **the Lord of hosts is His name; and thy Redeemer the Holy One of Israel; The God of the whole earth shall He be called. Isaiah 54:5 KJV**

Through our growth and understanding of the Biblical meaning of and our actual application of His Word, the fruit of joy with gratitude may be released from within; ***His abundance created in us***. What will be our ***choice***; to be ***Abandoned into Abundance*** or remain ***Abandoned in Divorce***? In adoring gratitude and praise, with sincere acceptance and love, shall we not arise from the ashes? He did promise to never leave or forsake us; NEVER ***Abandoned by God***. Shall we focus on the negative or rejoice in the positive; trusting in our eternal Husband Who never ***Abandoned in Divorce***?

> To appoint unto them that mourn in Zion, to give unto them beauty for ashes, the oil of joy for mourning, the garment of praise for the spirit of heaviness ... Isaiah 61:3 KJV

But for God! Are we refusing to ever attend another fellowship because we were de-fellowshipped; ***Abandoned by our Church***? In our personal relationship with God, are we not ***His abundance created in us***? We, that would include you, are the church; the body of Christ with its many members! Does not Jesus define who His church is, and not others? Being ***Abandoned by our Church*** may have exposed us to lessons about agape love that the visitors to the structures referred to as church building, are still not grasping; tutorials on love, forgiveness, compassion, acceptance and mercy.

> *Forgive us our sins,* for we also *forgive everyone who sins against us*[a] ... Luke 11:4

> *... thou shalt love thy neighbor as thyself.* Matthew 22:39 KJV

Meeting God face to face through His Word, let us allow Him to inform us as to whom we are in Him through ***His abundance created in us***. Through our personal failures, do we still not accept that God never fails us, but rather, envelopes us, you and me, His church, in His arms? Setting our paths straight and subsequently giving us the desires of our hearts, are we still not ***choosing*** to recognize the ***abundance*** of His grace bestowed upon us? Is this not the same grace that we each are to give back in performing ***His will to be done on earth as it is in heaven***? ***Abandoned into Abundance***, let us ***receive*** and be His new command; to love as we have experienced His agape love, ***His abundance created in us***? Jesus, our Groom, has promises to never leave or forsake His Bride, the Church. He will guide us, and never ***Abandon His Church***.

> *⁷ ... he that is without sin among you, let him first cast a stone at her ... ¹¹ ... JESUS SAID unto her, NEITHER DO I CONDEMN THEE: GO, AND SIN NO MORE.* John 8:7, 11 KJV

> *For this God is our God for ever and ever: he will be our guide even unto death.* Psalm 48:14

But for God! Is it impossible for God to heal the circumstances that resulted in us physically, mentally, emotionally or spiritually **Abandoning our Children**? If we have asked God for forgiveness then we are well on the way to receiving **His abundance created in us**; if we **choose**? Have we asked our children for forgiveness, and forgiven ourselves, or are we encaged in **condemnation**? Jesus' death on the cross eradicates the burden of sin. As we confess, our sins are forgotten and **removed as far as the east is from the west**.

> *As far as the east is from the west, so far hath he removed our transgressions from us.* Psalm 103:12 KJV

> *Therefore, there is now NO CONDEMNATION for those who are in Christ Jesus.* Romans 8:1 (Emphasis supplied)

As we await the healing return of the love of our children, let us immerse ourselves in fulfilling our purpose; **His will to be done on earth as it is in heaven**. The strength of His peace will undergird us. Let us commit our children to God as we may have done on the day they were christened or dedicated to the Lord. Let us wait on, trust in and have confidence in God to perform His perfect work in us and them. We are here to fulfill His purpose; **His will to be done on earth as it is in heaven**. Let us be **Abandoned into Abundance** rather than to remain caged in the **condemnation** of **Abandoning our Children**. Let us arise in adoring gratitude and praise for our ABBA Father's agape love, ***His abundance created in us***, His children. Let us ***receive*** the truth found in the words of His promise to never leave or forsake us; NEVER ***Abandoned by God***.

But for God! Cannot God forgive ***ALL*** sin? Yes, ***God can do all things***. He can even forgive us for the sin of our ***choice*** to ***Abandoned by Abortion***. Through God's infinite mercy and grace, we may receive His forgiveness and learn to forgive ourselves by ***His abundance created in us***. Just as God washed away all of David's sins, many of us today need to get out of the stagnations of our reality and become refreshed and renewed, physically, mentally, emotionally and spiritually. If we have confessed our sins, then our wrongdoing are in the past; remembered no more. Shall we not leave the events surrounding that conception behind; confessed and washed in the blood of Jesus; now removed by Him "***as far as the east is from the west***"?

Jesus has seen our tears. We cannot bring that child back. Let us be ***Abandoned into Abundance*** and not remain under the ***condemnation*** associated with our ***choice*** of ***Abandoned by Abortion***. For when God looks at us now, does He not see us as white as snow? If God remembers them no more then so shall we purpose to remember them no more also. Omniscient, omnipotent, omnipresent God knew. ***ALL*** things work together for good for ***His will to be done on earth as it is in heaven***. He has promised to never leave or forsake us. Nothing will separate us from His agape love; never ***Abandoned by God***. If we are to receive our healing, we will need to continuously apply His Balm of Gilead. Our Restorer cannot do this part for us. By renewing our minds by meditating on His Word day and night, we shall be freed from the ***condemnation*** of ***Abandoned by Abortion***. Let us receive ***His abundance created in us***; ***Abandoned into Abundance***.

> ³⁸ For I am persuaded, that *neither death, nor life, nor angels, nor principalities, nor powers, nor things present, nor things to come,* ³⁹ *nor height, nor depth, nor any other creature, shall be able to separate us from the love of God, which is in Christ Jesus our Lord.* **Romans 8:38-39 KJV**

But for God! We have a free will! Why do we want to select the *choices* that will cause us to abandon hope; to become *Abandoned by Self*? Yes, we may have planted some unruly wild oats within His intended Fruit of the Spirit gardens. However, the Word of God and time will be the best pest control to eventually destroy these blasted weeds of torrent. Should we relinquish the almighty power of God, *His abundance created in us*, and the fulfillment of our divinely ordained purpose to remain shackled by melancholy? God's message, should we *choose* to *receive* it, is the unyielding healing power of His spoken Word to empower us to no longer be *Abandoned by Self*. He longs for each of us to arise in praise and adoration, and in gratitude of Him and His *abundance* bestowed on us.

> The thief cometh not, but for to steal, and to kill, and to destroy: *I am come that they might have life, and that they might have it MORE ABUNDANTLY.* **John 10:10 KJV**

There is life or death in the power of the tongue Are we going to be *defeated*, *Abandoned by Self*, or *victorious*, *Never Abandoned by God*? What are we going to listen to; what are we going to say; what are we going to pray? Let us take the Word of God and hide it in our hearts; meditating on it, renewing our minds with it, and professing and proclaiming it; *Abandoned into Abundance* and not *Abandoned by Self*. Arising in *gratitude*, let us live victorious Christian lives for the entire world to see; for all the world to see Christ in us, our HOPE of glory. *His will be done on earth as it is in heaven*; never left and never forsaken; never *Abandoned by God*.

But for God! Have we *chosen* to live beneath the many guilt producing words and actions of our now adult children; *Abandoned by our Children*? As we await the power of God's outstretched hand to fashion His will in our offspring's' hearts, let us each adjust our focus, and set our positions on performing *His will be done on earth as it is in heaven*! Let us purpose to rejoice in and over the simple, uncomplicated matters of life; *His abundance created in us*. Let us catch sight of those that are placed in our daily paths; divine appointments to fulfill His purpose. It is amazing what bounty our Jesus truly lays before each of us when we endeavor to fix our sights on Him. Refusing to travel down *Condemnation Lane*, let us steady our course on *Positive Blessings Avenue*. Forgetting what is behind, what had to be broken to get us to this place wherein *we became new, let us press on*!

> *[12] NOT THAT I HAVE ALREADY ATTAINED, or am already perfected; BUT I PRESS ON ... [13] ... I do not count myself to have apprehended; but one thing I do, forgetting those things which are behind and reaching forward to those things which are ahead, [14] I PRESS TOWARD THE GOAL for the prize of the upward call of God in CHRIST JESUS.* **Philippians 3:12-14 KJV**

Should we not see the fulfillment of God's healing within our children on our earthly sojourn, we may still accomplish His purpose for His will to be done. We have a *choice*! We can hence forward allow His kingdom come on earth through the expression of Who He is through us to the broken and hurting world that surrounds us. Our journey's pain may be just the tools the Master has bestowed on us to perform that task in expressing His agape love. Let us thank God for His promise to never leave or forsake us; never **Abandoned by God**. In the midst of a potentially perplexing journey, let us leave the rubbish behind and press on to do **His will be done on earth as it is in heaven**. Do we desire to be **Abandoned into Abundance** or to remain in the misery of being **Abandoned by our Children**?

> *[10] Hope deferred maketh the heart sick: but when the desire cometh, it is a tree of life ... [19] The desire accomplished is sweet to the soul ...* **Proverbs 13:12, 19 KJV**

Remember, omniscient, omnipotent, omnipresent God knew how the pattern of the weave in each of our respective life's tapestries would be fashioned. They are ever hanging in heaven in perfect completion from the beginning of time. **But for God**! Forgetting what is behind, and what had to be broken to get us to this point, we press on! We are set *free* from the bondages of **Abandonment** into the **Abundance of God**, if we choose! Whom the Lord has set *free*, is *free* in deed for we are *new* creatures in Christ; all things become *new*!

> *If the Son therefore shall make you free, ye shall be free indeed.* **John 8:36 KJV**

> *... if any man be in Christ, he is a new creature: old things are passed away; behold, all things are become new.* **2 Corinthians 5:17 KJV**

God is in control, and by faith, we may begin to see His miracle of restoration in each of our lives. What has God called us to do today, or yesterday, or maybe it will be tomorrow? As we grow in His grace and knowledge, will we begin to flourish and not shrink? As we trust Him, the weeds of doubt and fear and lack of forgiveness will soon be plucked from each of our ***abundant*** gardens of life; allowing God to accomplish His divine purpose. We are His tools in evidencing ***His kingdom come on earth as it is in heaven***. Already broadcast in heaven, we are to obey His will on earth. We are to radiate through His anointed power, Christ in us for all the world to see. ***All*** things work together for good to those who are called by God; ***chosen*** by God! We are the ***Chosen***; never alone but rather Abandoned ***into Abundance*** to go and bring forth fruit!

> *... because God has said, "Never will I leave you; never will I forsake you."*[a] **Hebrews 13:5b**

> *... And surely I am with you always, to the very end of the age.* **Matthew 28:20b**

WOULD YOU LIKE TO BE A CHILD OF GOD?

For God so loved the world that he gave his one and only Son, that whoever believes in him shall not perish but have eternal life. **John 3:16**

Would you like to be forgiven of ***ALL*** your sins and start over with a clean slate? Would you like to receive this free gift of Salvation, paid for by Jesus Christ with His blood shed on the cross?

If you have not, as of yet, received this free gift of Salvation, the principally most liberating free gift you will ever receive in your entire life, let me tell you a little more about it.

You see, SALVATION as translated from the Greek means Savior, one bringing salvation, one who delivers, one who rescues from great danger or peril, one who provides healing, protection and preserves. This is a description of what the Gift of God is, and found only in Jesus. God's grace through Christ death provides you and me with this free gift that is both beneficent and redemptive to our personal welfare now, and for eternity.

So you have a ***choice***, my friend. So let me ask you again, would you like to be forgiven of ***ALL*** your sins and start over with a clean slate? Would you like to receive this free gift of Salvation and forgiveness of sins, paid for by Jesus Christ with His blood shed on the cross? Read the following verses and hear what God says to you:

> *For all have sinned, and come short of the glory of God;* **Romans 3:23 KJV**
>
> *For the wages of sin is death; but the gift of God is eternal life through Jesus Christ our Lord.* **Romans 6:23 KJV**
>
> *Jesus saith unto him, I am the way, the truth, and the life: no man cometh unto the Father, but by me.* **John 14:6 KJV**

> *If you declare with your mouth, "Jesus is Lord," and believe in your heart that God raised him from the dead, you will be saved.* **Romans 10:9**

If you would you like to ask Jesus to forgive you for ***ALL*** of your sins? Pray with me now:

> Lord, I am a sinner. I have lived my life my way and have made a bit of a mess of things. I want to receive your free gift of Salvation through Jesus Christ. I want Your everlasting life and love. I confess ***All*** of my sins to You. I am truly sorry. I can no longer do this on my own. Please forgive me for ***ALL*** of my sins. Please come into my life and take over. Please make me your child, and lead and guide me. Thank you Lord that Your Word expresses that if I confess my sins, You are faithful to forgive me of my sins and cleanse me from ***All*** of my unrighteousness. Thank You Lord for Your mercy and forgiveness.

And now, as a child of God and through His power, and your obedience, the love of Christ, your Savior, may be expressed through you for ***His kingdom come on earth as it is in heaven***.

It is that expression of His love through us that can reach out and touch all those around us. Will we be His eyes, His ears, His hands, His arms, His heart, for those who are ***abandoned***; for those who are seeking a sound mind though God's Word? Never ***Abandoned by God*** but rather ***Abandoned into Abundance***. Never forget His promises:

> *… because God has said, "Never will I leave you; never will I forsake you."*[a] **Hebrews 13:5b**
>
> *… And surely I am with you always, to the very end of the age.* **Matthew 28:20b**

Printed in Great Britain
by Amazon